The secret to good writing is to write good sentences, sentences that make a reader want to read the next sentence and the next one and the next one in the hope that they might learn something; not something about the writer but something about their own sweet selves. There are not many writers who can do such a thing. Amy Hayes evidently is one of them.

—Robert Benson
author

Amy Gaither Hayes says she's "not a writer" (like the rest of her entire family), but after reading this book, I see that she had no choice. I hate clichés, but this time it looks like the apple really didn't fall far from the tree.

—Mark Lowry
musician/comedian

This is not only a well-written book but also an excursion into a passionate soul. Amy Gaither Hayes helps the reader remember the wonder of that which too often is considered ordinary in our everyday lives and helps those who have lost a sense of blessedness in life's relationships to recover an awareness of their preciousness.

—Tony Campolo
professor emeritus of sociology, Eastern University

In *A Collection of Wednesdays*, Amy Gaither Hayes has helped me to recover some of my own memories of long ago events and dear people, memories I had almost allowed to slip away forever. Because of her words, I want not only to remember better but to see more clearly the preciousness of ordinary days as I live them.

—Peggy Campolo
speaker/writer

God speaks to us through the parable of our lives, but we need to be taught to listen. Amy's *Collection of Wednesdays* is just such a primer. As she speaks so eloquently from the overflow of her listening, she encourages you and me to do the same.

—Michael Card
musician/author

A Collection of Wednesdays

Creating a Whole *from the Parts*

Amy Gaither Hayes

ZONDERVAN®

ZONDERVAN.com/
AUTHORTRACKER
follow your favorite authors

We want to hear from you. Please send your comments about this book to us in care of zreview@zondervan.com. Thank you.

ZONDERVAN

A Collection of Wednesdays
Copyright © 2010 by Amy Gaither Hayes

This title is also available as a Zondervan ebook.
Visit www.zondervan.com/ebooks.

This title is also available in a Zondervan audio edition.
Visit www.zondervan.fm.

Requests for information should be addressed to:

Zondervan, Grand Rapids, Michigan 49530

Library of Congress Cataloging-in-Publication Data

Gaither Hayes, Amy.
    A collection of Wednesdays : creating a whole from the parts /
Amy Gaither Hayes.
       p. cm.
    ISBN 978-0-310-31895-8 (hardcover)
    1. Christian life. I. Title.
BV4510.3.G35—2011
248.4'—dc22   2010028322

All Scripture quotations, unless otherwise indicated, are taken from the Holy Bible, *New International Version*®, *NIV*®. Copyright © 1973, 1978, 1984 by Biblica, Inc.™ Used by permission of Zondervan. All rights reserved worldwide.

Any Internet addresses (websites, blogs, etc.) and telephone numbers printed in this book are offered as a resource. They are not intended in any way to be or imply an endorsement by Zondervan, nor does Zondervan vouch for the content of these sites and numbers for the life of this book.

In chapter 12, the lyrics of the song "I Believe, Help Thou My Unbelief," copyright © 1975 by Bill and Gloria Gaither, are reprinted by permission of Gaither Music Company.

Published in association with the literary agency of The Nashville Agency.

Cover design: Michelle Lenger
Cover illustration: © Istockphoto
Interior design: Michelle Espinoza

Printed in the United States of America

10 11 12 13 14 15 /DCI/ 19 18 17 16 15 14 13 12 11 10 9 8 7 6 5 4 3 2 1

For
Andrew
Lee
Madeleine
Simon—
Who help keep things whole

CONTENTS

DISSOLVING

As happy as I have been
there is no moment happier
than when I dissolve,
like the sugar in my tea,
melding into the stuff of my life,
its people, its sky, its earth —

the whole becoming all
and I am no longer one part
but part of one —
>   *the grass filling the patches next to my drive*
>   *the rain falling, noticed, into the pond*
>   *the egg and flour and honey into the batter*
>   *the music, interpreting the silence*

I grasp at this,
my most happy place,
where lost, I'm found.

WEDNESDAYS:

AN INTRODUCTION

I come from a family of writers—folks who can't go a whole day without writing. Folks who process everything with a pen in their hands. Folks who think nothing of calling one another while the kids are coming home from school and the dog is barking and the furnace repairman is hollering from the basement, simply to ask if you have a minute to listen to something they wrote.

In a sense I am like them, but in another I am not like them at all.

I am not a writer, not in the way that they are. I can go weeks without writing a thing, bothered by nothing more than the twinge of guilt you might feel when you think of a thank-you note you haven't written yet. I'm the only one in my family who doesn't write songs, and I've been working on my current journal for more than five years.

I write lists, of course, like most people who are trying to keep a five-person house organized and running smoothly. I write for my students at the university where I teach. I write the occasional article for my mother's magazine, if she asks nicely, and the occasional poem.

I am not One Who Must Write; I am One Who Can Write When She Must.

Apparently, for the last couple of years, I've needed to.

When I'm not writing, my life is plenty full. I teach part-time at a university. I try to act in plays once or twice a year, and I sometimes direct and help with costumes. I spend time with my family. Sometimes people ask me to come speak to them. I fix meals and clean messes and do laundry and go to meetings and run errands and take naps and read books and take walks and check email and play games and make phone calls.

In other words, I do what millions of other people do every day.

But as almost anyone will tell you, what you do is not the best definition of who you are. And that, in part, is why I started writing.

I write on Wednesday mornings. This involves coffee, silence, and the space to think, process, and create. This also means snail's-pace progress, especially allowing for interruptions like summer, Christmas break, and three kids who may be home from school with the flu.

Yet a picture is emerging. Writing about puzzles, and the joy of creating a picture from the disparate pieces, I connected with the idea of integrity—that wonderful word that means "wholeness." I'm writing to be able to say, as Shakespeare phrased it, "It's all one": the way I live, speak, dream, write, and grow.

My desire is that these Writing Wednesdays have

sketched a picture of something good, purposeful, and even beautiful. Take from these stories what you need to begin your own picture. We are, after all, the sum of our choices—a collection of Wednesdays.

MORNING SPENT

there isn't time
to write what needs to be written
a paragraph or a
chapter ... the deadline approaching
not even time really for a poem
but here it is
hurry
it's almost time to get in the car
and pick up the little one
and another one sick on the couch
the morning—dedicated, originally—
spent holding her head and
on the phone with the credit card
company, trying to solve a mystery
even the time it takes to choose a
font
hurry
searching for a simile:
what is it like?
It is like I went to a place
I've always wanted to go
and all I came back with
was this poem.
I've tried to make it
as humble as I could
and besides:
isn't my son coming out of

preschool a poem?
isn't holding my daughter's head?
isn't this popsicle unwrapped on the
first really spring day—
isn't everything?

PASSION

Several years ago at Fiumicino Airport in Rome, I witnessed an amazing drama. A young couple stood together in the security line. They weren't making a scene; they *were* a scene. Tears ran down their faces as they shuffled silently through the interminable line. Their hands were interwoven, or shaking, or enfolding the other in one more embrace. The boy bent and kissed the top of her head, her forehead, the curve of her ear, and she pressed her face into his chest as if trying to join her body with his.

No words needed to be said. In their last few moments of bodily presence, touch became their language of love. Each step brought them closer to each other and closer to the gate.

The boy was tall and lanky, his dark curly hair the kind that any mother would long to run her hands through. He carried one bag: a scuffed guitar case covered with stickers from all over the world. The girl was small; she seemed artistic and intelligent. She carried only a small shoulder bag.

Soon they were forced to separate. They kissed a final time, still crying silently, and then he walked through the security archway while she moved aside to watch him.

Was she Italian, and had her parents forbidden her to be with this American? Was she engaged to someone else? Was he destined for a place she could not follow? I felt a powerful impulse to run after him, to beg him to stay and make this true love work. What could be more important?

Instead, I kept walking. I didn't feel I could intrude on what seemed like a sacred moment.

The boy looked back to where the girl stood against the wall. Even as he walked toward the gate, their eyes were a lifeline across the growing waves of passengers. He turned the final corner; she remained leaning against the wall, her gaze fixed on the place where he had disappeared.

The whole place seemed heavy with her sadness.

• • •

The word passion has lost much of its original fire, but it continues to burn for me. If I am ever asked to be on my favorite television show, *Inside the Actor's Studio*, I won't need even a moment's thought when James Lipton intones, "And what is your favorite word?"

When I studied for my MFA in acting, Paul Steger taught Movement for the Theater, and Stage Combat. Paul is small, wiry, and charismatic, and many of us who came through that department had a crush on him. In one of my first classes with Paul, he said *passion* was his favorite word. It startled me because, like many Americans, I associated passion exclusively with sex. Paul explained that people who live with passion about their lives, their work, and their relationships were the kind of people he sought out. It didn't much matter what they were passionate about, only that they were, he said, because so few people are animated by true passion.

In my second year of study, Paul Steger and Kevin Hofeditz, another of my acting teachers, went to the University and Regional Theater Association (URTA) auditions, the place where most graduate theater programs recruit new students. After watching nearly three hundred auditions, they returned to school with a shortlist of five candidates.

Five?

I'll never forget what Paul said: "Those were the only ones with something going on behind the eyes."

In other words, in that crowd of aspiring actors, fewer than two percent were fueled by passion.

● ● ●

Passion comes from the Latin *pasi* — "to suffer" — a description of Christ's crucifixion. Christ's life *was* suffering, and His death was the pinnacle of that pain. Living with passion — true passion — requires living with pain. The opposite of passion may be comfort or, as John Eldredge suggests in *Waking the Dead*, apathy. Yet it is only by living passionately that we, like Jesus, discover true joy—a depth of wonder and fulfillment unimaginable to those who refuse to risk.

My mentor, Ann, was concerned that I not confuse passion with drivenness. Quite right. We don't need to be doing everlasting more. Passion is about quality, not quantity. A life of passion contains space and quiet because it is based in an awareness of God's passion for *us*. If our busyness makes us unable to appreciate this reality, we aren't living.

We're simply coasting. Spinning.

In the first scene of the movie *Hook*, Peter's wife cautions him that his kids are growing up, that *his* life is happening all around him whether he engages it or not.

"You," she says to him, "are *missing* it."

● ● ●

Several years ago I directed a community production of *Romeo and Juliet*. The reasons that made it foolhardy were also my motivations: the perceived inaccessibility of Shakespeare; staging a tragedy instead of a comedy; producing a four-hundred-year-old play in a largely uneducated, blue-collar, economically depressed community not known for supporting the arts.

Still, I was confident. As the ancient Greeks knew, tragedy can heal. It didn't hurt that *Romeo and Juliet* is a perfect play. Structurally, dramatically, emotionally, and spiritually, it's a ripping good story that will be performed for centuries to come. My director's notes began with a lyric from folk troubadour David Wilcox:

"Though there's evil cast around us / It is Love that wrote the play."

The play sold out. Audience members laughed and cried and wrote letters to the editor urging people to attend. During one performance, an older couple in the front row talked to each other the entire time, becoming more and more passionate about the plight of the young lovers as the play progressed. When Juliet woke in the tomb and found Romeo dead beside her, she grabbed his dagger. Visibly shaken, the woman in the front row gasped and cried out, "Good Lord, that poor girl isn't gonna kill herself too, is she?"

Romeo and Juliet were naïve and headstrong, and perhaps their love would not have lasted had their lives been spared. Yet what makes us uncomfortable, in this world so often void of passion, is the blinding conviction and fierce commitment of this young love. We cannot bear to look at a Juliet who chooses, at the cost of her own life, to follow another soul. Romeo's definition of love shines into the shadowed alleyways of our own poor convictions, echoing most nearly the love of Christ.

But there they are onstage, burning in all their glory. In the end, we cannot bear to look away. Beyond prejudice, beyond fear, beyond self-preservation or societal pressure or even life itself, we find in Romeo and Juliet the potential that lies sleeping in each of us: to love and be loved with unblinking ferocity.

Each of us waits, like the sleeping Juliet, to be awakened by our Lover's compassionate kiss, to be awakened by a Lover who has already died and lives now to love us.

I am a believer in this Lover. I too wait for Him to come and awaken me. I believe in Him with passion. And all of these experiences got me thinking. How many believers did I know who really believe with passion and, because of that belief, live with passion? Not very many. In fact, I realized, I know lots of people who just survive and scrape by, but don't really live with passion. And here I am in the arts, a field of study and work that is supposed to be based in and on passion, *and* I am a believer in the God of the universe, and I am His daughter. Hadn't I, of all people, better be a person of passion? I decided right then and there that I would be a person who lives with passion, and that I would allow God Himself to be the fuel of that passion.

MAKING SOMETHING

Unannounced, it all returns:
the faint murmurings, the clashing of swords
the play, the music, the young lovers
the longing for this to go on forever.
I close my eyes and see it:
the balcony
the gossamer robe
the long rehearsals
the young bronze skin
the tears after the wedding
lit behind a scrim—
the color red and shadows
of a chalice, a binding stole, a dagger.
"Ah, happy dagger, find
your sheath here in my breast!"
There is a desperate ecstasy in making something.
It enters, plants its seed, and dies.
It leaves a ripe and full emptiness.

BAM

i was doing morning chores and
checking mail when a
poem escaped.
i had thought i would finish
a few things
drink some more coffee
maybe grab a bite before the later
whirlwind when bam —
i had to
stop
altogether
and let it out before it hurt me.
so this is it i guess
not much i suppose
but enough to stop me cold
and consider this morning
before the fast train
how much i owe
to poems to stopping to the words on a page and
to the whole shining day before me.

2

CALLING

When I was ten, soon after Christmas when the last strands of lights were still clinging to eaves and hedges, my parents took me to see *Annie* on Broadway. I remember nearly every detail: the hush of the audience when the orchestra tuned up for the overture; the singsong way Annie called to her dog, Sandy; the bright red color of Annie's dress in the finale. I returned to school the next week able to recite every line and relive every shining moment, taking up my entire music class with the report. To this day I remember that night, though some of the details have faded from memory.

It was the night I received my calling.

Our seats were in the third row of the orchestra center section. Weeks earlier, my mother had given me the cast album, and it wasn't long before I knew every word of every song. During the show, I perched on my seat, rapt, my whole being transported onto the glowing stage.

After the show, we went to Mama Leoni's, the popular after-theater Italian restaurant in midtown

Manhattan. I bubbled over with talk about the show, scarcely able to order or eat. A strolling violinist who was wandering the room made his way to our table and asked if I had any requests. I immediately shouted out " 'Tomorrow!' " — the hit from *Annie* that everyone was singing and no one yet hated.

"I'll play it if you'll sing it," he replied, chuckling.

Before he could reconsider his offer, I jumped up on my chair. The violinist gave the introduction, and I began to sing. No, I *belted* out the words. The restaurant grew quiet, whether in surprise, embarrassment, or admiration I'll never know. When I finished — "it's only a day a-waaay" — the room erupted in a standing ovation. The violinist bowed to me as I took my seat, beaming.

I knew I'd just seen my future.

After the meal, my parents took me on a carriage ride through Central Park. It was nearing midnight, and our breath made glistening clouds in the icy air. I snuggled between my parents under a warm blanket and fell asleep, but not before watching the snow begin to fall across the park. I dimly remember my father carrying me into the bright lobby of the hotel, up the elevator, and laying me in my bed, where I dropped into sleep like the final, resolving note of the orchestra.

I cannot think of that night without feeling again the shimmering magic of knowing who God had created me to become.

Acting is supposed to be an unstable profession,

full of dangers and pitfalls, but I never feel so safe—so solid and so *me*—as when I am working in the theater. The stage is where I know myself.

The stage is where I rest—like I did that winter night between my parents—knowing that my God-given dreams are mine to follow.   —

ACTING

Fitting like corn on rural route #1
Replete like rain-soaked wool
Decadent like past-ripe peaches
True like God
Frightening like a dream
Incarnate like a laughing child
I roll in it like wet grass:
It evaporates like poetry
Clinging like the mist
On Denmark's dark castle

GREEN

Today I discovered my eyes are not green!
I sat in the bath with a mirror,
the light from the window streaming in,
and there, in plain sight, were my eyes:
blue, with gold flecks.
I stared, not comprehending.
All my life, I thought they were green.
They've been green like the pond,
like the grass underfoot: solid, dependable.
Then, just like that:
Blue and gold.
The splotches in an impressionist painting,
mixed not, it turns out, by God,
but by the viewer, by the eye.
Here, in my fortieth year, I sit blinking,
Unable to face the truth.
Jeez. Just when you think you know someone.

3

SAND

My family has vacationed in Nantucket roughly every other summer for the last three decades. I was three the first time. Family friends introduced us to the island off the coast of Boston; they had been to Martha's Vineyard — Nantucket's more famous, commercialized cousin — before falling in love with the quaint, quiet beauty of Nantucket.

We have countless memories buried on Nantucket, like so many horseshoe-crab shells on the seaweed-strewn beaches. One memory, now almost sacred in its recurring beauty, is our sunset picnic on Dionis Beach. We seldom visit this beach during the week we are on the island, preferring to wait until the final night at sunset, when it is at its loveliest.

Most days, we eat breakfast at one of the wonderful island diners or bakeries while the fog is still hovering over the ocean. By midmorning, it usually has burned off, and we know what kind of weather we will have for the day. If it's cloudy or rainy, we go shopping or stay in and play games and do crafts from the suitcase full of materials my mom always brings with her on vacation.

If it's sunny, we decide which beach we will bike to. There are several to choose from, but we have our few favorites. Jetties Beach, with its wide expanse of sand and shallow waters, is good for sunning, sand castles, and swimming. Surfside is for those adventurous ones who want to beat up their bodies battling the waves. The Children's Beach is small, easily supervised, and has a large jungle gym right on the beach for the little ones.

By the end of the week, we are tired from all the biking and playing in the sea and also a little sad at the thought of leaving the island. We pack the cars with picnic supplies, guitars, footballs, and buckets for shells and head out to Dionis in the early evening. Dionis is beautiful for lots of reasons, including the fact that it is textured with picturesque sloping dunes topped with tufts of sea grass. Situated as it is on the west end of the north shore, it also boasts spectacular sunsets.

The parking area is down behind the dunes, so when we pull up and unload our supplies, we must all help haul everything up and over the dunes to find a good picnic spot. It's usually a bit warm with the sun still up, and by the time we've climbed that last hill, we are hot and tired, but the first sight of that beautiful ocean with the sun sparkling on it like diamonds always takes away my breath. The breeze that the dunes block now blows coolly in my face, and I have the sense that we are someplace familiar, beloved, and welcoming.

The big kids have always loved spending the first hour or so jumping off the dunes into the fine sand below, while the adults and the little ones comb the beach for interesting shells, bits of seaweed, and hermit crabs. When everyone is hungry, we spread out our picnic and eat, reminiscing over the week and the years of memories we have in this place. The guitars come out and we sing just about every song we can think of, and when the sun dips its last sliver of fire into the ocean, we pack up and say our goodbyes, remembering the way the ocean always looks as we crest the dune for the first time.

● ● ●

Several years ago we introduced our friend Kristi to the ocean. We were staying in Gulf Shores, Alabama, and we flew her down to meet us in Pensacola. We asked her to keep her eyes closed on the drive to our beachfront condo. She changed into her bathing suit, walked across the sand with my hand over her eyes, and then stopped. I pulled back my hand. She gasped, squealed, and then sprinted to the water, scooping it up and tasting it. She yelled, "It *is* salty!" We laughed and laughed, delighted by her delight.

A few years later, I heard Amy Grant tell a story as she accepted an award for influence in faith, given at a ceremony in a cathedral in St. Paul, Minnesota. She told a story almost identical to ours, about introducing her nieces, who had never seen the ocean, to the Gulf. She too drove from the airport to the hotel, not letting them peek, until she walked them to the beach, at which point they screamed and ran straight into the water in their dinner clothes. Amy said, "I feel like that's what I get to do: introduce people who have never known God to the vastness of his love. And it is such a delight and a privilege and so humbling to get to be the one. Thank you." And she accepted the award and walked off the stage.

I never see the ocean without thinking about her words. I think about the way Kristi squealed when she saw the ocean for the first time, and about how it looks when I walk up over the dune in the late afternoon at Dionis. And I think what a joy it is to experience that vastness, that awe, that delight for the first time, every time.

● ● ●

So many times over the years I've tried to write about my feelings about places like Nantucket, about Dionis Beach, even about my childhood home, but it just ends up sounding like a travel brochure rather than the love letter I intend it to be. What is it about a place that stirs the soul so? What is it about certain places that feel familiar even though I've never been there? Why do some places cause the heart to beat faster in anticipation of the unexplored, even though I've been there a thousand times? What causes me to long for Another Place, when I love the place where I am? My preacher grandfather, and perhaps C. S. Lewis too, would say that my hunger for Another Place is spiri-

tual, that because we are pilgrims here, we will always
long for Another Place and search for the home of our
hearts. Perhaps certain places have something about
them that speaks to us of this other home, this home
of the heart.

I am restless by nature. I don't claim this is a good
thing. I am often praying that God will make me content where I am. But perhaps part of my restless nature
is a gift, a burr under my saddle, so to speak, to keep
me alert, aware, awake, and interested. Maybe I am not
meant to be comfortable with how things are all the
time. It's such a difficult balance: to stay grounded and
content, at home in Jesus, and also pay attention to the
nudgings of the Spirit. I don't pretend to have it figured
out, but I wonder if my restlessness pushes me to look
for clues to what this other home is like.

●●●

When we step off the ferry on Nantucket and
hear the gulls calling and the fishing boats coming in
for the morning, and smell the salt in the air and the
clam chowder from Cap'n Toby's on the pier, I have an
immediate emotional and physical reaction: memories
of thirty-three years of alighting from the ferry flood
my mind, and I feel a rush of excitement and peace,
and anticipation. It is all familiar and wonderful, but
it is not home, exactly. Home is landlocked in the flat
cornfields of Indiana ... isn't it?

Or is home on another stretch of beach I've
adopted, the one where my husband grew up? Is it the

long wait in the bottleneck on highway 59, the endless stretch of road to that first glimpse of the Gulf
after the last stop back at Burris Fruit Market for the
week's supply of ripe tomatoes, corn on the cob, and
Chilton County peaches? My mind begins to unwind
and I stretch my car-tired muscles as we unfold kids
and bags and groceries out of the van and that first
blast of Alabama July hot hits, and mingled with it the
Gulf breeze and a hint of fried seafood. Here, the sun
doesn't sear; it *seeps* into my aching joints like a heat-
ing pad; it's too hot *not* to relax, and I know the salty
warm water is waiting to cradle me as I float in that
infinite expanse of sea. But these are sensations added
to my already full bank of memories, built on another
family's traditions, and while I've come to love every
moment of it, it isn't home either.

●●●

I begin to wonder if there is something to the idea
that we respond in these ways to these places because
we are built with a homing device, as it were, that
recognizes elements of our true home when we see
it. These elements can be anything from the smell of
good cooking, to the sound of the waves on the shore,
to the way my little son's arms feel as they wind themselves around my neck. Something in me responds
with, "Yes! I remember this!" even if it's the first time
it has ever happened. Similarly, an experience I've had
many times, like cresting the dune at Dionis, feels new
and extraordinary because it is a preview of the sights,

the sounds, the feel of coming Home for the first time. In that Home, time, as we know it, will cease to have any bearing on our experiences; everything will feel like the first time at the same time that everything feels familiar. This is how we can feel at home when we are in exile, and how we can feel displaced when we are home.

● ● ●

When I was a child, my mother used to pack a small package of plaster of paris in her suitcase. She'd take a bottle of tap water and a sand pail to the beach. She'd mix the plaster in the pail, lead us to the wet sand at the water's edge, and make plaster casts of our feet. She has them still, on the shelves of the book-case upstairs in her house, feet of all sizes cast in sand and plaster. She has written on the bottoms of them in black permanent marker whose feet they are, what our ages were when they were cast, and at what beach they were made. But I can tell this last detail without looking. If the foot is covered in brownish, coarse sand with bits of shells, I know we were in Nantucket. If it is fine white sand, I know we were visiting a beach somewhere along the Gulf in Florida. I have similar little feet on my bookshelves, made with my children on our beach trips.

I'm beginning to guess why my mother started this rather strange little ritual. It was partly to mark our growth and preserve precious memories, yes, but it was something else too. It was to remind us as we walk through this life that we may never feel completely at home here. That though we will search for and find adventure, explore and delight and make memories and discover all that is Other, we will never rest completely or ever find Home until our journey here is done. Then as we crest the hill and see that sparkling vastness for the first time, it will be utterly, completely new, and we will know it is Home.

LEAVING NANTUCKET, LATE AFTERNOON

Flying west from the ocean
certain mysteries apply themselves
like fog to my salted skin;
My children drank this air,
pure once, into their lungs
for the first time,
cupping the picture of the lighthouse,
the memory of the long bike ride,
like the saltwater they tasted
in laced fingers, tiny oceans
of cold sipped and spit out,
faces split by grins.

I'm tired suddenly and want to cry.
What did I start out to write?
A poem, maybe, or a ballad.
A poem, Loves, about salt:
how it wrinkles my tongue,
how it stings my hot skin,
how it seasons us all,
leaving us cured and thirsty.

SCRAPBOOK

She made books for years
books for us
books full of us
our faces work stories.
One year the books were full
and faces clippings words began
appearing on the door
the back door
the door through
which we all everyone
pass, going out or
coming in.
Others' faces too, and scraps
of their lives caught
by graduation photos
Christmas card pictures
and newspaper clippings.
So that the door became
a tapestry the
threads of which were
pictures faces words
of us all of us anyone
who touched us or
passed through our lives
through our door.
Through time they seemed
outdated seemed old seemed
like clear that off make
room for something new.

But she never did she
never cleared only layered
adding taping and pasting
over like pages of a
book no one can open
only glimpse through, through
behind around beyond.
So now they seem both old
and new present now
time weaving in and out
like faces like people
passing through the
book the door the tapestry.
She leaves it there.
Children grandchildren friends
swinging opening on its
hinges welcoming
in and ushering out:
a practical scrapbook.
I think I know why
she did it
because we pass through it
and there we are
there we all are.

4

CHILDREN

I wrote a poem when my oldest son, Lee, was almost two. In it, I described his rage at catching me watching him play. What mother doesn't love to watch their child play? He was so imaginative, so funny, so sweet. But if he caught me, boy, did I catch it. I didn't know at the time what a reflection of his personality his behavior was: private by nature, desperate to be respected; he gets so angry when his dignity or respect is put into question. I'm still learning about him, but one of the things I'm learning is how little I know.

Actually, the more I parent, the less I know about it, so if you're looking for help or advice, you'd better go look in the self-help section of the bookstore. I've read more than my share of that kind of book in the last six months, and while I learned a great deal from each of them, I also figured out I won't be writing one of those books anytime soon. I am also learning that my husband, Andrew, and I can't do this alone. I need other people, preferably those who have gone before me, raised a kid or two, been there, done that, and aren't afraid to kick my butt when I would rather run than fight. And I've never prayed more, leaned more, asked for wisdom more, or generally cried out for help more than I have since we've entered the teen years.

I was an easy child. Ask my mother. I thought disobeying was just avoiding the inevitable, rebellion was for stupid people who had time to waste, and outright defiance was suicide. Add to that my horror of rocking the boat or engaging in debate, and you have a very compliant child. Fast-forward thirty-five years, and you have the makings of some pretty serious turbulence when that child has to grow up and start parenting a very strong-willed child who, to make things even more challenging, absolutely lights up at the prospect of a good fight. I thought everyone, under the surface, probably felt mostly the same way I did about things. Enter Lee.

We weren't very far into this parenting thing when I realized I was in way over my head. I spent hours at our church's altar, surrounded by older and more experienced mothers who rubbed my back and handed me tissues while I sobbed, "You have to help me with this child before I kill him! Or he kills me!" He was three at the time. I remember feeling that way during labor: that moment when you realize with horror that you can't actually do this thing you started in bliss nine months ago, plus however many less-than-blissful hours you've been counting through contractions, and you want *out*. Of course, by that time, there *is* no out. The baby's coming, maybe even crowning, and there's no way out but through.

So it is with parenting. What started out as sleepless nights and sore breasts segued right on into endless lunch-making and mess-cleaning, but I still thought I had at least a grasp on how to do this and do it well, no matter how tired I was. Then we hit the teens. Everything I thought I knew evaporated in tears and frustration, leaving me to realize this is the most important part and I can't go *anywhere*. On the contrary, this child who used to have a healthy fear of me and who now made it quite clear that he neither wanted nor needed my help in anything, actually needed me more than ever. Talk about confusing. And I thought natural childbirth was hard.

But I think that might be the point. God seems to specialize in putting us in situations in which we feel inadequate, for which we are unprepared, and through which we must depend on Him. I'm beginning to think He does His best work then, when we are very clearly out of the way. And obviously I do not have it all together here. Paul says I should be praising God when it's like this; God is strongest when I am weak. But weakness is just really hard on my sense of capability and control.

●●●

Now, before I get carried away, let me say this: Lee is an amazing kid. He is on his way to becoming a wonderful man. He is gifted, talented, intelligent, philosophical, charming, spiritual, handsome, funny, well-liked, and quite mature for his age. He's just challenging, but most exceptional people are. (Not that Lee is the next Einstein, but can you imagine having *that* kid in math class?) The thing is, I'm slowly realizing that many parents would not find him challenging at all. They might, in fact, find him quite a breath of fresh air. But he's a challenge for me, and so I often find myself whining to God, "Why did you give him to *me*? Isn't there someone else suited to this particular job?" But, obviously, God gave him to us for a reason, and so He must know there is something particular that only I can teach him, and there is something particular that only Lee can teach me.

Just when I thought I had this parenting thing down, I am learning so much in these new waters. I've learned from books I've read, from experts, from wise parents God has sent my way, from my own parents, and from the hard way: by trial and error. It's a wonder any child makes it to adulthood not stark-raving mad. But by grace and some miracle, most of them do, in spite of us and our well-intentioned efforts. Eugene Peterson in his book *Like Dew Your Youth* says that God gives babies to young adults to teach them that they aren't the center of the universe. He gives teenagers to middle-agers to teach them that they aren't done learning. I can testify to that.

A wise woman I met recently said to me three things she had heard from God when her son was younger and difficult: "You have authority over this child because I have given it to you. You will never make him happy by giving him everything he wants.

You can do all things through Christ who strengthens you." I asked her to repeat them so I could write them down. I've seldom heard anything more straightforward, more true, or more helpful in regard to parenting.

I am also learning to relax a little, which is hard for me, because I have basically two gears, parentally speaking: comatose and frenetic. I either find myself burying my head in the sand when behavior frightens me, or overreacting to the point of feeling like I'm becoming Amanda Wingfield in *The Glass Menagerie*, wailing, "I've become hateful to my children!" Please, God, no. I've also realized how much fear has marked my parenting, and I am still dealing with that, but I am reminded again and again that "perfect love casts out fear." A fearful approach to parenting, or anything else, points clearly to a lack of love. I pray for more love, for grace, for understanding, for strength. If all else fails, I pray for the guts to believe the words on a notepad my mother sent me: "Never underestimate the power of a hissy fit. Some things are worth the fight."

● ● ●

I must rest in God's arms, knowing that my children are tethered, that they have been dedicated and reared and placed in His hands, and I must learn to trust Him. The process, as my friend Ann is fond of reminding me, is very often the whole purpose of the journey. And everyone's process is his or her own, unique, and God-accompanied. I find that I am really good at trusting God with just about everything except my children. But that, it turns out, is the one area in which I really have no choice. They will go their own ways, they must hear their own names called, and they must answer with their own voices.

A few years ago, my two oldest were baptized at the church we attended at the time. I wrote this piece to commemorate the occasion.

> Easter. A fitting time, I think, for baptism, that wettest of mysteries which somehow symbolizes cleansing and being born at once. At least these are the words I use as I struggle to explain to my children why we do this, what the ritual means to us, and what it symbolizes for them and for the church.

> I am both eager and anxious for Saturday's service; while I've witnessed many baptisms in my life, only one has been of this sprinkling variety. The liturgy of baptism is new to me; so is our church's method. But I am eager for another reason.

> I watched and helped as Lee and Madeleine wrote statements of faith this week, struggling to articulate their understanding of this symbol and their choice to participate in it. Lee's expressed his desire to participate in communion. While I am ambivalent about our new church's position on baptism in regards to communion, I am delighted communion means so much to him. Madeleine simply stated she "felt

in her heart it was time" to be baptized, following only by a few months her conversion.

I wonder if either of them — if any of us — is aware of what else will take place as their heads are sprinkled with water and their foreheads marked with the sign of the cross in olive oil. Traditionally, a baptism and a christening were one: that is, a baby received both his assurance of eternal life (in the face of the strong odds of infant mortality) and his name. Today, of course, most babies come to their baptisms with their names already firmly bestowed, and adults at their baptisms aren't renamed. Yet I wonder.

I think of the account of Jesus at His baptism, performed by John. When He emerged from the water, the heavens opened up and a dove settled on Him as a voice from heaven declared, "This is my son, in whom I am well-pleased." Surely God was leaving little doubt for those present as to who this Jesus was.

I don't expect such a dramatic occurrence at my children's baptisms. But I can't help but hope that some part of their hearts will open as the water trickles down their scalps and into their eyes, and they will hear a still, small voice calling them by their names, their true names, naming them as only the Father can do, and sending His pleasure in them to settle deep in their hearts. I pray that, like Mary Magdalene at the tomb, they will hear their Lord speak their names, and in a flash they will recognize Him and know at last who they are, marked and sealed by the cross.

—Easter Vigil 2003

Sometimes I read it to remind myself that they are on their own paths. We started them on their paths, but at some point, we must let God be the loudest voice in their lives.

So that's about it, really. All I know about parenting at this point.

This would have been a much longer chapter a year ago.

DELIVERANCE

"Reach down and pull out your baby"
I feel the slick underside of your arms
strong and full of rhythm
I recognize their bony elbows, jabbing wrists and search-
    ing fingers
from the months of muffled movement
I hold tightly, carefully
my fingers meeting at your spine
as the rest of you wriggles free of its prison
like a butterfly emerging from its cocoon
I feel the awesome emptiness below
the familiar fullness above
as I pull you to my breast
and the nourishment here begins
shoving the old nourishment out and away
You make your entrance as confidently as you began
assuming there is room for you here
assuming your mother will catch you
Now the burden of you has shifted
and you make your demands on others
Your father severs the last connection to your old life

For a moment the veil has lifted

HIDE AND SEEK

My son shouts his protest as he discovers me
watching him work on a tower
I know I must learn other methods of surveillance
become adept at observing him
employ the ways of the underground mother
He squeals when I pounce from behind the table
We begin the chase
laughing
once again, it is a game
I know what comes next
his exits, alone
his attempts and growths and sins
I won't be allowed to watch
I crouch behind the table
listening for his movements
understanding at last this rehearsal

DINNER

I was once asked by a magazine to write about what I learned from my mother. That's a pretty big assignment for one article, but the more I thought about it, the more I decided that what my mother taught me, besides almost everything, could be summed up in one word, or more precisely, one meal: dinner.

Well, not just dinner. Breakfast too.

Let me back up. My mom is famous for being well-spoken and for being spiritually very wise. She is infamous, in our family, for one phrase in particular. She often refers to, in the course of almost any conversation, the importance of "finding the eternity in the moment." While we have heard this so many times we have almost stopped hearing it, it is probably the life concept that she has most effectively taught me. What she means by it is that we must look at each moment, each occurrence, each person, with the perspective of eternity. What does this moment mean in the grand scheme of things? What can I learn from this person? What might God think about this event? What jewel of eternity, what gift of heaven, is hiding in this seemingly mundane or difficult or horrible or secular happening? Think of it as a big-picture approach to life. It's a tricky concept, and one that I believe takes a lifetime of practice to perfect, but as philosophies go, it's not a bad way to make sense of life. I'm not sure she was aware of it, but she taught it to me best through doing things like making the beds, washing the dishes, and fixing dinner.

Now, lest you think I am one of those content-to-stay-home, submissive, and domestic types who love nothing more than to know what's for dinner every night a week ahead, preferably made ahead and waiting in the freezer, think again. I am, after all, my mother's daughter. I am most happy when engaged in passionate discourse about matters great and small, philosophical and theological, global and local, with anyone from my colleagues at the university to the guy who comes to fix the furnace. My life is as hectic as yours, and although I am peace-loving, I am anything but meek.

But I am a nester. I've always loved creating an inviting and at least mostly peaceful home. I'm not a bad cook, and both Andrew and I find cooking stress-relieving. I come from a long line of good cooks on both sides, so it's no great shock that I'm at home in the kitchen. What I am pleasantly surprised to discover, though, is the sheer delight I am developing at creating good meals for my family. I don't mean just the nutrition part, although that becomes more important every day, as my kids' bodies grow and the general nutrition quality in restaurants and at school diminishes. What

I'm talking about is the quality of conversation at the table, the interaction at the end of a busy day, and the simple rest of sitting, eating, and talking.

Also, I came up with a way to take the time to really read Christmas cards and share them with my family. Early in the year, we put a basket near the dinner table full of all the Christmas cards we received last year. Each night at dinner, each person takes one out and reads it — the whole thing — to everyone at the table. When each card has been read and admired, with the time and attention we never have during the Christmas season itself, we pray for each sender or family and ask God to bless them this year. We usually finish them all sometime in May.

Other times we talk about our day, how relationships or classes or tests went, or what our plans are. Sometimes we dream together about upcoming trips, places we'd like to go, or things we'd like to do. Some nights, I'll be honest with you, we are each too tired or preoccupied to talk much at all, but that's okay too. We are together, breaking bread, being nourished, and at least we're tired together, in the same room at the same time, even if it's only for twenty minutes or so. These days, that may be the most I see my teenager all day.

●●●

I learned this from my mother: how to create a meal and a place for sharing it that encourage lingering, exchanging ideas, and laughter. Like my mother, I usually have a centerpiece, often seasonal. I always lay out placemats. Sometimes I put on music. Most nights I light the candles. When my kids were little, I taught them that when the candles are lit, we are reminded that God is present. It's also a reminder, as my mother might say, that every day and every dinner are a celebration.

Breakfast is less fancy, usually eaten at the counter (three stools for three kids). But I learned from my mother that sending kids out into the world to serve God and "develop moral muscle," as she calls it, requires training and preparation. Sending them without prayer and Scripture is like sending them out into the cold without coats. So once the biscuits and bacon or cereal and boiled eggs are served, and the lunches made, I sit in my red chair by the fireplace to read a story from *Egermeier's Bible Story Book*—simple enough for my seven-year-old to understand, and detailed enough to keep my twelve-year-old's interest.

Now that my oldest is a young man, he doesn't usually join us for breakfast, and so my prayers for him are silent, usually prayed while I am making his lunch or waiting to hear him come downstairs so I can hand him his bagel before he runs out the door. I figure I have put into him what I can, and now I must daily put him into God's hands and pray that he hears that still, small voice above the din of his peers and his culture.

By the time the younger ones' teeth are brushed and their coats are on, in the midst of all the hustle and hassle, I feel that at least I've filled their bellies with something good and their minds with something, well, eternal. And these are the things, I hope, they will remember when it is their turn to prepare and send kids out into their world, whatever the world looks like then. Of course, the world will continue to change, and change rapidly, but it is my prayer that my kids will be trained, as I was, to spot the eternity in every event, in every person, and in every moment.

●●●

My kids aren't always appreciative of these things right now. They might roll their eyes when I bring out the Christmas card basket, or complain when I ask them to set the table correctly, or argue that they don't have time for the reading this morning. But I do it anyway, because I believe it's worth it. I think too that I do it with the hope that they will think back to our home when they are out on their own and that they will smile, remembering a feeling, a warmth, and a desire to create a place of peace. I do it hoping they will realize that those memories were created with effort and with love. I do it hoping that they will want the same feelings, even if they aren't the same memories, for their own families. I do it hoping they will be able to discern the difference between real and false, solid and temporary, quality and quantity. I do it hoping that they will one day recognize a glimpse of eternity in the quotidian acts of making the beds, washing the dishes, and eating together. And I do it to honor my mother.

THE BEGGAR

Sitting on the counter
He tips his pink cup forward
I slice strawberries into a bowl
Carefully cutting the green tops from the soft flesh
He pursues his quest for more
Employing charm and whatever it takes
He gets what he wants
He presses the berries into his mouth
Sucking at escaping juice
Peering into the empty cup before tilting it for me to see
I fill his cup with the red coins
He empties them, filling his hands, his mouth
Like the words that fill him
Leaking out messy, flavorful
Their stain a mark on my heart
I watch him discovering
His eyes opening to the treasure in his cup

HOW TO SEE

Coming away from it,
I wonder how to see it:
specifically, the parts extracted and studied,
or whole, the details receding into a wash of color and
    light.
Even the frame materializes, a possibility,
setting the picture against the comforting wall of entirety.
Or should each gesture, each comment, each character
be lifted out,
held so the light passes through,
illuminating subtext as though they were cherished pieces
of Laura's menagerie?
Later, the searchlight of my memory
sweeps over the event
and my place in it—
Lighting here and there on a face, a smile, a fear, a
    peace.
I turn off the light,
releasing the stillness which covers it all
like water filling a boat,
pulling it down,
pulling it toward silence,
pulling it toward peace.

6

REST

On my mother-in-law's refrigerator is a short script I wrote:

> **Martha**: Jesus, Mary won't help me and there's so much to do! Can't You make her help me?
> **Jesus**: Martha. Don't just do something. Sit there.

My mother-in-law, Janean—everyone calls her Luv—has taught me a great deal about both doing and sitting. She just about reaches my shoulders, and her black eyes and dark hair (think Snow White) shine as she moves with quick, graceful purpose. I'm pretty sure she can do anything: she plays piano; she cooks fast and furious; she sews; she destroys any crossword or sudoku puzzle you hand her; she visits prison inmates; and when she brings down a buck, she donates the meat to her local homeless shelter. Children adore her, men are drawn to her, and women want to be her. She's soft-spoken and pretty, introverted and fearless, and the term "Steel Magnolia" doesn't even begin to describe her.

●●●

It was late July in Alabama, and we were all down at Horses Horses, the family farm where Andrew's parents built their big log home south of Birmingham. Luv and I were arranging wildflowers in vases in front of the huge hearth. Above the big stone fireplace is a thick chunk of heart-of-pine that serves as a mantel. Busy arranging the flowers, I stood without thinking and banged the back of my head. I didn't pass out, but I saw stars. Luv stopped working and said, her thick Southern accent full of concern, "See it?"

"No," I gasped through tears. "I *didn't* see it!" What a strange thing to ask me—of *course* I didn't see it!

"See it!" This time it was a statement, firm and direct.

"No!" I shouted, frustrated. "I didn't!"

Luv reached up and grabbed my shoulders. "See-it *down*," she commanded as she shoved me onto the couch, "before you pass *out*!"

We laughed so hard that we *both* had to see-it down. It's vital to know when the work should stop and the sitting down start.

While Luv is almost always busy, usually in the kitchen, and sometimes plays the martyr, what she understands in her experience and maturity is when to stop. When Luv leaves the kitchen, she sits in the living room with us, and her focus is on us, on the children, on whatever is happening in the room at the moment. She might have been Martha a moment ago, banging pots and pans in the kitchen, but she seems to know when it's time to become Mary. She stops her Martha routine—"Lord, why am I doing all the work?"—her eternal doing, and shifts into being mode, into Mary mode. She chooses the best part, and "it will not be taken from her," according to Jesus. This is what I long to learn from Luv, this ability to know when it's time to stop, to sit, to be.

● ● ●

I am as much of a frantic doer as the next guy. I get caught up in checking one more thing off the list, cramming one more thing in before the kids get home, and in the process missing the moments when they *are* home. Worse, I miss the presence of God Himself most of the day. And then, when I lie in bed at night, exhausted and aching, my mind chides me with the things on the list that I didn't get done, rather than rejoicing in the things that I did and in the peace of the evening. It's an insidious disease, this desire to do more without thought of being. It's as eroding as cancer.

I read something by Thomas Merton once that I was never able to forget, try as I might. He called "activism and overwork" a "violence" that the modern world practices on itself. We do it by "fighting for great causes" and through "rush and pressure." He calls this kind of activity a "frenzy," and he says that by allowing ourselves to be pulled into it, we negate all the good that we are trying to do by "killing the root of inner wisdom which makes work fruitful." He should know: he left a normal, busy life sometime in the 1940s and became a Trappist monk—the most austere and lonely of all monastic lives—in order to learn about prayer, silence, and stillness.

I know about this violence. I fall prey to it every day of my life, and I feel it in my soul and my body. I have experienced illness and crisis because of the pace at which I have tried to live. I have woken up on beautiful mornings, looked into the bright eyes of my children, and felt the barren landscape of my own inner life staring at them from my lightless eyes. I have worn myself out trying to work myself into the presence of God by studying, praying, going to another Bible study, working on one more committee, volunteering at school, teaching another class. I know that faith without works is dead, but I also know that works without the life and joy that oneness with God brings is death itself.

This violence is taking its toll on us all. Not just in our bodies, although hospitals are full and pharmaceutical companies are rich from the illnesses we bring on ourselves with too much stress, too little sleep, and no time for being. Our souls are also suffering. Churches are full of burned-out, overburdened, and resentful workers who go home more burdened and heavy-laden than they came. We had a pastor who once said in a sermon that we had traded the cross for a treadmill as a symbol of our salvation. Ouch.

●●●

On the wall at the top of our stairs I had a friend paint a poem by seventeenth-century poet Sir Thomas Browne. The speaker suggests we empty ourselves in order for God to fill us with Himself, and offers a reminder of where all our "shrewd activity" takes us:

If thou could'st empty all thyself of self,
Like to a shell dishabited,
Then might He find thee on the ocean shelf,
And say, "This is not dead,"
And fill thee with Himself instead.

But thou art all replete with very thou
And hast such shrewd activity,
That when He comes He says, "This is enow
Unto itself— 'twere better let it be,
It is so small and full, there is no room for Me."

Things were pretty much the same four centuries ago: "But thou art all replete with very thou." Or as we might phrase that now, "You're so full of yourself!" To be replete is to be full to the point of saturation, like a sponge full of water—full in a way that begs to be squeezed out, emptied, lightened. In the fullness of ourselves, we are small, because there is no room for God's fullness, a fullness to which there is no end.

My grandmother had a theory about the fullness of God. She called it the Thimble Theory. She said everyone will be filled in heaven, and that when we are in the presence of God, we will be filled with His

glory *to our capacity*. For some, that will be a thimble-
ful, and for others a huge vat. Our capacity is deter-
mined by how we deepen and grow here on earth. Full
is full, Grandma said, but if she had a choice between
a thimble of glory and a vat, she was going to go for
the vat!

Picture a hole in the damp sand. Going deeper
requires stillness and care; a rush of constant effort
will collapse the hole time and time again. Sometimes
we live like we believe that bumper sticker: "Jesus is
coming — look busy."

● ● ●

I speak to groups about rest, busyness, and the
struggle of living a contemplative life. One planning
committee preparing to host me suggested I use a
word other than *contemplative*. They suggested some
cute, catchy titles for my talk, like "Our 24/7 God"
and "God and Me: The Primer." I'm not big on cute.
I like simple, direct, to-the-point titles like "The Contemplative Life." In fact, after contemplating how lame
their titles were, I politely insisted on my contemplative title.

Finally, they admitted the problem: half the committee didn't know what contemplative means. I
thought of a new title for my talk: "How to Use a Dic-
tionary." The planning committee had provided me
with just the illustration to prove my point: how could
a group of apparently mature Christians in leadership
positions not know what contemplative means?

To its credit, that committee did some research on the word in advance of my visit. They discovered the Native American belief that a person, the self, is like a house with four rooms. One room is the physical (the body); one the spiritual (the soul); one the intellectual (the mind); and one the emotional (the heart). If a person doesn't visit each room every day, they aren't really living in their house. How many of us live in only one or two rooms of our houses? How many rooms are *never* lived in?

Most Christians have heard about the discipline of "having a quiet time" or "doing devotions." There are plenty of books and methods that will tell you when, how, and where to do this. I distrust these methods. Anyone who tells me that I'll be holier if I talk to God first thing in the morning has never been a mom with three kids. I need a quiet space of about thirty minutes, and that's in the afternoon, while Andrew and the kids are still at work and school and Simon is down for a nap.

Here's a confession: I don't just take time alone to read. I nap. I'm a napper. Ever since college, I try to lie down after lunch and rest for about twenty or thirty minutes. My grandfather did it every day for fifty years and lived to be ninety-one, still traveling with my dad to manage the record tables. (Incidentally, he got more work done than men half his age.) I'm much more effective the rest of the day if I take a break from it, and you can ask my kids: I'm a much nicer mommy.

Why this makes me feel guilty, I'm not sure. I can only surmise our culture doesn't reward rest, and so we are a bunch of overachieving, underslept, and overly stressed people. Why I don't move to a country like, say, Italy or Spain, where the entire country takes a nap every afternoon, I cannot say. They sound like godly places to me.

Actually, I think many effective people take naps. The book *Having Our Say* was written by two sisters who lived to be in their hundreds. The oldest one wrote a sequel to it when her sister died called *On My Own at 107*. In the first book, they talk about their parents, who founded and presided over one of America's first African-American colleges, all while raising ten or eleven highly effective, pioneering children. They say, though, that their mother took an hour for herself every afternoon in her study, and that no one was to interrupt her while she was in there. She probably read her Bible, wrote in her journal, things like that. But I'll lay a wager that she sneaked a little nap in there before reemerging to change the world. How else could she manage?

● ● ●

Before my nap, I read. When I speak to people about this, I encourage them to be discerning about what they read for their spiritual deepening; if it isn't nurturing you, nourishing and challenging you to growth, stop reading it and find something that will. Read and meditate on Scripture. For me, that means one or two chapters of a book, with time for notes, thoughts, and pondering. Find a system for reading the Bible if you aren't sure how to start; one way is to read one chapter of the Old Testament (you can start at Genesis), one of the New Testament, and one psalm every day. Or you can get a lectionary, which cycles through the whole Bible every three years, and read passages each day.

Right now, I tend to read whatever I'm studying with the college girls I disciple or the high school girls I'm doing Bible study with. (We're finishing Esther today over tea.) During the summer, when all the students are off, I'll read whatever book of the Bible I feel addresses what God is working with me on. (I usually ask my mother for suggestions.)

Then I take some time to pray. I pray about people, family, and world situations, for guidance, about decisions, for my children and my husband, about things that are bugging me — everything. Sometimes I image a prayer, which is to say I picture the person or thing or situation and hold it up in my mind's eye to God. I picture Him taking it from my hand and filling my hand with His instead. For instance, if I'm worried about one of my kids and I don't know how specifically to pray for him (do we ever know?), I picture holding that child up to God and allowing God to take him away from me and hold that child.

There is a way to pray with every breath you take, a way practiced by the contemplative abbas and ammas (or desert fathers and mothers) who lived in isolation in the Egyptian desert during the first several centuries after Christ. I close my eyes and focus on the breath entering and leaving my body. As I inhale, I think the words, "Lord Jesus Christ," and as I exhale, "Son of God." I breathe in again—"have mercy on me"—and out—"a sinner." I continue to breathe, and this ancient Jesus Prayer rises with the rhythm of my chest.

Prayer is deeply personal, and each of us needs to find the time and space to share our own words and thoughts with our Creator. Anne Lamott says there are really only two prayers: "Help me, help me, help me" and "Thank You, thank You, thank You." That sounds about right. Anyway, as my favorite Scripture passage points out, it's okay that we struggle with how to pray, because the Holy Spirit prays for us: "In the same way, the Spirit helps us in our weakness. We do not know what we ought to pray for, but the Spirit himself intercedes for us with groans that words cannot express. And he who searches our hearts knows the mind of the Spirit, because the Spirit intercedes for the saints in accordance with God's will" (Rom. 8:26–27).

● ● ●

Have you ever caught yourself frozen in time, staring into space, not really thinking about anything, but just being? Perhaps when you are filling the tea kettle at the sink, or looking for something in the kids' room? It's a moment of clarity unlike any other, except maybe that moment before sleep, when your thoughts are pure and free and untangled, and your focus is simple and full. Obviously, we can't live that way, staring into space. But wouldn't it be something if we could access that purity, that stillness, in the midst of our busy days?

I seem to have these moments most with my children. I'll be busy folding clothes or making down the bed, and I'll realize that my son Simon is telling me something. It might be about some scene he imagined his Bionicles having, or a girl at school he "just can't stand" but he never seems to talk about without smiling. And all at once, I'll stop what I'm doing and look at him, and there it is: clarity. I'll see everything about him: his eyelashes, the slope of his nose, the velvety skin of his cheek, the way his sandy blond hair falls in chunks over his high forehead. But I see not just what he looks like. I'll see the urgency and earnestness of his need to communicate what is happening in his head, and the fact that he will never again be the age he is right now. I'll know beyond a shadow of a doubt that sometime within the next seven years, he will begin to shut me out, turning inward as his need to process new ideas and thoughts becomes more private, more introspective, and less dependent on my response. And I am present—maybe for the first time all day—really present in this moment. I am aware of what is happening at the same time that I am really tuned in to what he is saying to me, really listening to every word, every nuance, and everything he doesn't say.

Chinese theologian Watchman Nee compares this phenomenon to the Old Testament temple. In the outer courts, there was bustle and business; the temple teemed with activity and purpose that seemed, at times, hectic or even chaotic. But in the inner sanctuary, all was peace, quiet, and presence. Inside this sanctuary was the Holy of Holies, a fifteen-by-fifteen-foot cubicle in which the Holy Spirit was said to dwell. Only a veil — a thick linen curtain — separated this sacred place from the sanctuary and the bustle of the outer courts, but the difference was astounding. When Jesus died on the cross, and this veil of the temple was torn in two, not only were we invited into the presence of the living God, but His presence came into *us*. There was no separation. This place of peace, reverence, quiet, and focus came into us.

The stillness that existed inside the Holy of Holies now exists within us, a quiet sanctuary in which the Holy Spirit dwells. Outside can be bustle, business, laughter, and work, but inside there is stillness, with no ruffle in the veil. This is the stillness we are cultivating, and as we do that, something else happens. We become the place of peace.

I have been surprised often by people who come to our house in times of crisis because they say our house is so peaceful. I look around at the kids running in and out, the phone ringing, the dog barking, and think, Are they in the same house I'm in? Once, a girl we went to graduate school with appeared on our doorstep, distraught and weeping. She was someone I had admired, but I never felt that she liked me very much. She had been through a terrible heartbreak, and when I asked her why she came to us, she stammered, "Because when I think of peace, I think of you." She ended up sleeping on our couch for a couple of nights while she got herself together. We fixed gallons of iced tea, and while Andrew cooked and brought her tea, I listened as she poured out her heart, stunned that she chose us for this healing task. We came to realize it wasn't the house she found peaceful; the place of peace was in us. She was drawn to the stillness in the inner sanctuary, the dwelling of the Holy Spirit.

Catholic churches keep the bread and wine — called the Host because they become the body and blood of Jesus when blessed — in a box on the wall called the tabernacle. When the elements are in the box, a candle is lit beside it to announce that the Host is present. If I am the temple of God, how often is a candle lit beside me?

●●●

Raise your hand if you need to turn on the radio or TV when you are alone. Are you afraid of the silence? Afraid of God? Of yourself? I believe that our crisis of busyness and stress is less a crisis of time management and more a crisis of identity and relationship.

Donald Miller, in his book *Blue Like Jazz*, writes about his difficulty with the image of God as Father. His father left his family, and Miller didn't have a concept of a loving father by which to understand God. He thought that using the image of God as father was a "marketing mistake." Some of us don't have an earthly father; others have suffered under the hand of a father who was abusive. Still others had fathers who were present in body but absent in affection. Even those of us with good fathers, like mine, have a hard time imagining the kind of loving father God is. This, I think, is really the basis of the problem; we feel like we have to *do* because we don't know whose we are.

To live in the realization of our belovedness is, for various reasons, one of the hardest things to do. But to catch even a glimpse of it each day will change how you live your life. It will change how you see yourself, how you see others, how you see the events in your life. Why is being loved such a difficult idea to come to grips with? Is it because our idea of who God is is a bit skewed by our experiences? Perhaps we don't ever really get it, but perhaps we get a better idea with our own children.

If you have children, is there ever a time that they aren't precious to you? Do you find delight in watching them sleep? Do you rejoice when they succeed? Does your heart fall when they fail? We've just been through a particularly hard summer with our teenage son. My heart broke watching him struggle, make bad decisions, and isolate himself with the consequences of his decisions. Through all of this, I discovered more and more about how deeply, passionately, I love him, how I long to see him joyful, living in the fullness of righteousness, and how I ached for him when he failed. I nearly went crazy with love for him. Don't you think your heavenly Parent, lover of your soul, feels all these things for you and more? At the risk of sounding frivolous, He is crazy about you. So often, I wish our children would just stop running for a minute and let us hold them and love them. How often does God wish the same thing of us?

My sister Suzanne went through a dark and difficult time a few years ago. She struggled to hear what God was saying to her, and strained against His silence. She sat down one afternoon to read her Bible and pray. She had her journal, her pencil, her devotional book — all the props she thought she needed. She dutifully began to work when she felt she heard God say to her, "Just stop. Please stop." She stopped. She started to pray, when she felt Him interrupt her again. "Just shut up. Please. Let Me hold you. Let Me love you." So she sat, doing nothing, and closed her eyes, and felt the arms of God hold her. The coldness, the distance, the darkness, and the silence melted away. Tears streamed down her face as she allowed the Almighty to love her.

●●●

My grandmother gave me a great gift. I think I was about thirteen years old, a time when a kid's concept of herself is pretty well shaken. She called me into her living room one rainy fall afternoon. She had a fire burning in the fireplace, and she sat me down in her big wing chair and told me she had something to read to me. She brought out an old book with a tattered brown leather cover with gold lettering on it. She said it was an old poem by Longfellow, and that while she was reading it, she wanted me to think of the speaker of the

poem as God, and the girls in the poem as herself and
me. Then she read me "The Children's Hour":

> Between the dark and the daylight
> When the night is beginning to lower
> Comes a pause in the day's occupations
> That is known as the Children's Hour.
>
> I hear in the chamber above me
> The patter of little feet,
> The sound of a door that is opened,
> And voices soft and sweet.
>
> From the study I see in the lamplight,
> Descending the broad hall stair,
> Grave Alice, and laughing Allegra,
> And Edith with golden hair.
>
> A whisper, and then a silence;
> Yet I know by their merry eyes
> They are plotting and planning together
> To take me by surprise.
>
> A sudden rush from the stairway,
> A sudden raid from the hall!
> By three doors left unguarded
> They enter my castle wall!
>
> They climb up into my turret
> O'er the arms and back of my chair;
> If I try to escape, they surround me;
> They seem to be everywhere.

They almost devour me with kisses,
Their arms about me entwine,
Till I think of the Bishop of Bingen
And his Mouse-Tower on the Rhine!

Do you think, oh blue-eyed banditti,
Because you have scaled the wall,
Such an old mustache as I am
Is not a match for you all!

I have you fast in my fortress,
And will not let you depart,
But put you down in the dungeon
In the round-tower of my heart.

And there I will keep you forever,
Yes, forever and a day,
Till the walls shall crumble to ruin
And moulder in dust away!

She looked at me steadily and said, "I wish someone had told me that this is what God is like, that He
loves me like this. Amy, I want you to know that you
can climb up into God's lap, just like these children,
any time in your life — that He *wants* you to, and that
He delights in your attention and in you."

I'm not sure I understood the importance of what
she was telling me at the time, but the older I get, the
more grateful I am for her gift. Not just for the book,
although I still have it, with its cracked binding and
loose pages. I treasure it because it represents her
greater gift and because it is a reminder of who I am,

and of whose I am. It is a reminder that sometimes what God wants more than anything is for me to climb up in His lap, to rest my head on His chest, and to allow Him to love me. He wants me to stop running, achieving, doing, and just be in His presence, in this moment. And when I do this, the peace that comes as a result becomes a haven in which others find rest.

EARLY

No matter how early my alarm goes
off, it's not early enough to be
ahead, to get any work
done, because I fall in
love with the dark, the
quiet, the sounds of
coffee brewing in the stillness, the
lights of the Christmas
tree reflected in the black satin
window, the dog breathing slow on the
floor, the silence of my family sleeping
upstairs, the swish/hush of one or two
cars driving through the wet
street, and all that I love wrapped around my
sleepy body here on this soft
chair by the fire in the dark, stirring
early.

MORNING SYMPHONY

In the dark of this morning
I lie next to the small body of my son,
Whose breath was an opus.
I mean to say,
His breath whistled and sang like the heaving of an
     orchestra,
His body rising and falling like the conductor's baton.
It was dark, as I said,
And so I imagined his striped pajamas,
Covering the swells of this mighty orchestra:
All blues and reds and yellows
In a sort of dance
Of long vertical lines,
Swaying gracefully, sensually
To the strains of the symphony
That was his breath.
And then, the shadow of light began behind the trees,
As the music of my son's breath
Ushered in this day.
I lay there, listening.
Just then, he sighed, the strings and woodwinds
Stopping suddenly,
And then resuming their gentle cadence,
So sweet, so sure.

7

POSSE

At the university where I teach, a leadership honors program sends recruiters into inner-city high schools to identify groups of students with excellent academic and leadership abilities. These groups are offered scholarship money—the Posse Scholarship—to attend our small, midwestern school at which they can earn a top-notch liberal arts education. In return, the university is immeasurably enriched by the involvement of students who are something other than white and upper middle class.

In the past, individual students from the inner city who attended the university seldom stayed longer than a few semesters. When the university administrators asked one of these students his reasons for leaving, he answered simply, "Because I didn't have my posse." Consequently, the Posse Scholarship recruits groups of students from the same region, seeking to create an instant network and support structure for kids experiencing so many new changes simultaneously. With change comes challenge, and grounded friendships provide strength and confidence.

We all need a posse. I've ached for intimate, female friendships for as long as I can remember. I've had friends my whole life — acquaintances, people I enjoy seeing, coworkers, and so on — but rarely true friends. The kind who call each other for no reason, the kind who live close enough to keep in regular, face-to-face contact.

I did not have good luck finding true girlfriends in elementary or high school — at least not the kind that stick for life. I have one or two close friends from college and grad school with whom I keep in touch, and even feel very close to and share many stages of life with, but long distance, in between changing diapers, answering phone calls and emails, and seldom face-to-face. I had a dear and life-saving best friend all through middle and high school, but he was a boy, and after we went to different colleges in different states, and he moved to Chicago, we lost touch, even though I still love him and think of him often with affection and gratitude. I have a long history of finding *the one* only to have my heart broken by hurt, growth, or distance.

By the time I hit thirty, finding a faithful, present friend seemed unlikely, let alone a group of them all at once. I longed for the kind of intimacy that encompasses real life, from recipes to theology, from family life to clothes, and from shoes to our cosmic purpose. Could I find someone who would put things on hold to pray with me when I was falling apart, and who would, in turn, call me when she needed the same? I wanted desperately to be known — deeply, honestly — and loved because and in spite of that. And I wanted desperately for that friend to be someone other than my mother, who is required to love me come hell or high water.

Of course, God had something to say about all this: why did I so badly need to be loved by someone other than my family, my kids, and my husband? And more important, why wasn't God enough?

● ● ●

I gave birth to our third child. We moved to a new town and said goodbye to a woman I had come to love. I threw myself into our new community, getting involved at the kids' schools, meeting people at church, throwing parties, and trying to develop new relationships. I made lots of friends, and even one that I thought was the real, intimate friend I had been praying for. But after a series of misunderstandings and hurts, we pulled away from each other. I was heartbroken and confused. I asked God why, and all the while I waited, as lonely as I've ever been.

Every Scripture passage I read, every devotional I studied, every person from whom I sought counsel and comfort—all seemed to be gently prodding me to lean on Jesus. This should have come as no surprise, since I had long been praying for God to "crowd me to him," to quote Ed Miller's *Letters to Shear Jashub*. I felt like that little boy in the joke who, when he tells his daddy he's scared of the dark and his daddy tells him that Jesus is with him, replies, "I know he is. I just want Jesus with skin on."

I knew I wasn't alone. My family lavished love on me so well it took my breath away. I felt God manifest Himself in myriad ways. I just longed for Jesus with skin on, preferably in the form of someone who wanted to be a good mother and wasn't afraid to talk about how her love for anything with icing bordered on obsession.

Like I might say to my children when they don't get something they want, God seemed to say to me, "Yes, I understand what you want. It's a good and natural thing to want. You just can't have it. Not yet, anyway. Just put your head down, right here on My chest, and let Me love you."

"Yes, yes," I replied impatiently. "I know You love me. I know lots of folks love me. I know You are supposed to be enough. But aren't there many examples in Scripture of godly, intimate friendships? What about David and Jonathan? What about Ruth and Naomi? What about Mary and Elizabeth? What about all the great girlfriends my mom has? They wrote a book about it, you know. They go on tour and speak about it. What about all those chick flicks about female friends? *Beaches. The Lemon Sisters. Divine Secrets of the Ya-Ya Sisterhood.*"

"Put your head down," He said.

I really struggled. But I put my head down.

This went on.

I wondered what was wrong with me. People seemed to really like me, so why didn't that affection ever put down deep roots? Had we moved too much?

Was I drawn to the wrong kind of woman? Had I set my sights too high? Too low?

I think God purposefully kept me in that intense, lonely, and heartbroken place so that I would ask these hard questions, do the necessary soul-searching, and learn to be content with the love that was already being lavished on me. Not bad parenting, if you think about it.

Then a miracle happened—three of them, actually.

We called ourselves the Posse.

• • •

The four of us weren't smart enough to have organized things on our own, so we figured God did it. God saw each of us isolated in our loneliness, and knew that it was not good. He had, after all, created us to be in relationship with one another, to share each other's burdens and laughter. And here we were, struggling along on our own, each in her own pain and loneliness, longing for the Eden of companionship. And God saw it and said, no, it definitely was not good. So He arranged a meeting.

We were all in the same church and each of us had a fondness for the others, but the thing that finally pulled us together was the immigration of a woman named Laura. She, along with her husband and three daughters, had been a missionary in Africa. I've learned, through missionary friends, something of the trauma of readjusting to American culture, and I saw right away that Laura needed our help.

I reached out to the two other people I knew and trusted the most at church and asked if they would join Laura and me for lunch. We took care of picking the restaurant and ordering drinks, and God took over from there.

After church several weeks later, one of us sent one of our kids to find the other women, telling the child to say that "Mom's posse needs you." The name stuck, and just like that, the Posse was formed.

●●●

We were mother, peacemaker, party-planner, and sage, and together we were ready for anything life threw at us. One of us was curvy (not me), beautiful, gregarious, and had great instincts for people. One was quiet, reserved, and constantly surprised us with her wry humor and ornery tastes. One was small and scrappy with prophetic, razor-sharp observations and the gift of confrontation. I guess I was the ringleader, in that I love to plan a party and get people together, but other than the fact that I was definitely the loudest, I'm not sure where I fit in. But fit in I did, and it was very good indeed.

In The Lord of the Rings series, Tolkien creates a band of brothers who, in spite of or because of their differences, work together to save the world, looking out for each other as they travel and fight together. I want a band like that. I think about Elizabeth Bennet and her trusted sister Jane from *Pride and Prejudice*, or Celia and Rosalind, those closest of friends from *As*

You Like It, and I know that these women, like those, would fight for me, pray for me, look out for me. I liked the idea that while Laura was working at the bank, she was sending up a prayer for my healing when I was sick; that when Holly sensed a rebellious spirit in me, she loved me enough to point it out; that while Suzanne was helping her daughter learn to drive, she stopped by my house to bring me a flower to remind me I am precious to her.

I knew that we all would do this and more for any of the others. Once, when one of us needed to get out of a dysfunctional marriage, the rest of us helped her pack. Then we helped her move into a house and painted all the walls a cheery yellow. Another time, we took her teenage daughter on a shopping trip, in hopes she would open up and talk about what was going on in her life.

Many times, one of the women took my kids to school or picked them up for me when I couldn't get there in time. Once, when one of us was exhausted and working late, we all cooked dinner and took it over and set her table, so she could just come home and sit down with her family. We have stopped at each other's houses unannounced and in desperate need of prayer. We have counseled and been counseled. We have laughed until we've cried and laughed while we've cried. We have grieved and celebrated each other's losses and victories. And I know that any one of those women would go to the gates of hell to pull me back or chase Satan himself there to protect me. And I would do it for them.

Jesus traveled in a pack. He understood that humans need each other. He knew this world is too much to battle alone. Each of us needs "Jesus with skin on" to walk beside us through green pastures and dark valleys. Jesus, sent by the Father and led by the Spirit, defines community for us, and we His followers become a unified body that is both mystical and practical.

A friend of mine once said that being ministered to by the body of Christ — His followers — "turned her from a person of faith into an actual eyewitness." The body of Christ, our band of brothers or sisters, or both, is just that: the body. Jesus with skin on.

●●●

I don't know how long I'll get to "keep" any of these women. Two of them have moved away, and I've lost contact with one of them. It doesn't matter. Each one demonstrated the body to me in ways I never could have learned any other way. They turned me into an eyewitness. I am thankful for them, for their presence and witness in my life. And through them, miraculously, I am learning that even when I am lonely, Jesus is more than enough, with or without skin on.

TO NEW FRIENDS: A WARNING

You should know:
I must hold you carefully.
I often break what I try to hold,
Or I want it too much, hold it too tightly,
Crush it with my need.
You have slipped through my fingers
Or been released in boredom,
Like a doll I've played out.
I've turned my back, deliberately,
Hoping you would go away.
You did. I am not proud of this.
When I turn my passionate gaze on you,
Watch out. I have been known to burn with my
Wanting, my needing, my indifference, my forgetfulness.
I have been known to kill with neglect.
I have been known to dazzle and leave you breathless,
While I go somewhere else to rest.
I don't say when I'll be back. Performance is exhausting.
After all this time, I still don't know how
To do this well, this which seems to come so easily,
So naturally, to you. How did you learn it?
Some just seem born to friends, and keep them.
It is a gift I often ask for. You give me hope.
One day I may figure this out, and you may be
The one who gets to teach me. Don't listen too closely
To my warnings. Stay. I am an eager student.

LIFE LESSON

For Heather

The day you taught me to make iced tea
you were not happy with me
You felt like the only one
who took care of things And
who keeps leaving the pitcher empty
on the counter Fill it up
What do you mean
you don't know how
What kind of grown up doesn't know
how to make iced tea
You took me by the hand and
dragged me into the kitchen
You will learn now
two large tea bags
scoop of sugar
pour boiling water over
cover it with a towel
wait six minutes
fill it up with cold water
No more excuses now and I
better never find this empty
again
Seventeen years later I put the
full pitcher in the fridge, whispering
Thank you

8

CHURCH

We have a ministry at our house that's a puzzle. Literally.

It just sort of happened. My family adores jigsaw puzzles, and every few days we get one out and set it up on the library table. When we have a few minutes, we wander by and insert a few pieces. We talk about our days over a puzzle as we wait for dinner to be ready. Some people think we must not have a television. We do. We even watch it sometimes, but we haven't found anything on that competes with a good puzzle.

This is how we came to have a puzzle out during house church one week. Several of the folks wandered by to put a few pieces in and chat as they waited for others to arrive. After dinner, people ended up back in the library, fitting in pieces and waiting for the gathering to start. It was after the gathering that things really started happening.

A few of us had found ourselves back around the puzzle table. Heads together, intent on completing the picture, intimacy blossomed. Chatter became talk.

Talk turned into confidences and confessions. Prayer began.

In other words, church happened. And the Puzzle Ministry was born.

•••

I've been trying to figure out how it works. It's just a puzzle after all: a picture photographed or painted by someone, cut into little irregular-shaped pieces by a machine, and dropped into a box. But if we don't have one set up in the library before people arrive for house church, inevitably I hear someone call out, "Hey! Where's the puzzle?" as though I had forgotten to provide ice or forks or furniture or something.

How can a puzzle be such a force for creating community, bringing down defenses, and encouraging confession?

I think it must have something to do with drawing a small group of people, with their heads bowed and their eyes averted, all focused on a common goal: to make sense and beauty out of what seem like random and disconnected pieces. It sounds a little like communal prayer, if you think about it. There's no threat, no heat, just a companionable comradeship that allows us to be who we are as we face the challenge together of seeing the big picture, of making a whole of the pieces.

And this, I find, is the New Testament description of church in a nutshell: "They had a common goal, spending time together in confession and prayer, studying the scriptures, and sharing what they had with those who needed it" (Acts 2:44 – 45, my paraphrase). In the process, I suspect, they made something beautiful together. When I look at it like that, I think we must not be too far off from what Jesus has in mind. We've made a start, at least, even if it includes something as prosaic — or mosaic — as a jigsaw puzzle.

• • •

We meet with a group of people every Sunday night at our house — students from the university where my husband and I teach, folks from the community, friends and families we've met along the way. We're pretty loud for the first hour — that's when we eat. Everyone brings something to share, and there is always enough food that more or less goes together. In sharing what we have, we are communing, and trying to be authentic as a group.

We are trying to be the church. We don't always know what that means, but we want to learn. When it seems like we're feeling our way along in the dark, it's because we are. We have no church manual, and few precedents other than the New Testament letters to the churches and the book of Acts. Sometimes it's messy — we're messy, after all — but we are learning what it means to be real people. Not just during the week at work, or with our families, or when we are alone, but when we are in Christian community, which is harder than it seems.

• • •

Before doing anything else, we always eat together. Always. Before we try to settle down or listen to the Scripture or pray for one another or confess our failures, we eat, and it makes a difference. After sharing each other's homemade food, our defenses lower; we've probably laughed a good deal; we're full, comfortable, and putting up our dukes simply seems like too much work. It takes longer to do church this way, but it saves loads of time.

One of us is a retired widower named Vern. Vern is eighty-five and has one arm after losing the other one to a hay baler when he was a young father. Over time, Vern's presence has become less verbal. His memory isn't as good as it used to be, so he doesn't contribute to the conversation as much as he used to. But we feel his presence. Vern is cherished and revered, especially by the young people. We have several young adults who come to worship every week, and the longer they're here, if they're paying attention, they come to realize their part in helping Vern keep his place in our community. Someone will get him a chair; another makes sure he has something to drink after he's settled on his red stool by the kitchen, where he can greet people as they enter and where the little ones can easily climb up into his lap. At dinner, the young men jostle for seats next to him so they can ask him for tales about his experiences in World War II, or his early years as a farmer, or his love of the great Big Band music of the 1930s.

One of Vern's greatest friends is Adam. Adam is a

talented young man who has grown up without a dad, made some destructive choices, and has decided to end his downward spiral and pursue a relationship with Jesus. Even without a car or much money, he finds a way to our house every week to join us in our pursuit. Adam can be arrogant; he's good-looking and smart, but lately he's lost much of his cockiness as he comes face-to-face, week by week, with God's grace, mercy, and overwhelming love. Adam is a doubter who, like Jacob, demands a blessing. He's less concerned about the limp than about wrestling with what matters.

Last week, Vern wasn't at church. Adam went from person to person asking, "Have you heard from Vern this week? Why isn't Vern here? Do you think he's okay?" Does this qualify as miraculous, or even remarkable? From where I stand, watching a self-absorbed man, confused and lost, find his identity in the body of Christ is miraculous indeed. Adam is discovering what it takes some people years to learn: the shortest distance between yourself and joy is a straight line to others.

● ● ●

Vern's life has been difficult. Vern has dealt with serious disappointment and fear. When he lost his arm, he was a young man with a wife and four young children. He had already been through the war and all the horror and heartache that that entailed. Now he had to figure out how to support his family in some way that didn't require the use of both arms. He started his own real estate business, and after years of hard work, it became a reliable living. His wife was his partner and the love of his life, and when she died, he had to figure out how to live on his own without her help, which he did for many years. He's done his wrestling, and he's not escaped unscarred. I am sure there have been seasons of bitterness, anger, and fear in his long life. But there is seldom a moment he doesn't have a smile, a kind word, a gentle reminder, a wise remonstration. He's quick to laugh at a joke, to put someone at ease, to dismiss his own extraordinary history and remarkable outlook as nothing but the Lord's blessings.

The simplicity and generosity of Vern's spirit is a balm to all of us. He has many years of experience, which has helped make him wise, but he also has what experience is sometimes not enough to teach: he is very rich in faith. The debate is over for him. He has proved his faith in his Father over and over again, and rests joyfully and lovingly in the hands of God.

He also has a great sense of humor. He is always eager to tell an old joke or hear a new one. He has a hearty and generous laugh, and he is seldom without a grin on his face and an ornery twinkle in his eye. The occasional awkwardness caused by navigating with only one arm is easily and casually offset by his willingness to laugh at himself. Almost every week, my youngest child climbs up in his lap, pats the empty sleeve where Vern's arm should be, and asks to be told again the story of the hay-baling accident. Vern patiently tells him again how he lost his arm. "Does it still hurt?" Simon will always ask. "No," Vern will say, laughing. "It might if it were there, but it's not there, so it doesn't hurt." He is always interested in everyone else and in what is happening in their lives. No wonder a fatherless kid like Adam is drawn to him. We all are.

One time we met to worship during Advent. A discussion about the incarnation turned into a discussion about the need for redemption, which turned into a discussion about sin. My daughter, who was about seven at the time, looked concerned and suddenly spoke up.

"What's the difference between a sin and a mistake?"

Momentarily caught off guard, we all looked at each other, unsure of how to answer. Vern, however, never hesitated but leaned forward in his chair, cleared his throat, and told her in simple terms how he understood the matter. He said that a mistake is something that we all may do from time to time when we don't know any better or when we are not thinking carefully, like accidentally tripping someone who walks by because we didn't notice that our feet were in the way. A sin, however, is something that you know to be wrong, that you feel a definite pull *not* to do, but you do it anyway, like tripping someone on purpose, just to see them fall.

Madeleine nodded, relaxing a little. Vern seemed intent on helping her to understand that she couldn't accidentally sin and then be held accountable for that without her knowledge. He knew instinctively that

this, in her seven-year-old mind, was what was both-
ering her. We all watched them, Vern on his stool leaning forward to be able to see into her eyes, Madeleine
sitting at his feet gazing up at him, trying to understand what he was saying. We all held our breath, captivated by this scene of grace, the generations naturally
interacting with and drawing from each other. It was
a thing of beauty, a natural blossoming of the body of
Christ in action.

This is why we need elders. This is why we need
church.

●●●

Some mornings Vern drops by for coffee. When
our five-year-old sees "Mr. Vern," he always asks if
we're having church.

No, we're not, I tell him. And then I realize that
we are.

HOME CHURCH

The four of us trek together:
our oldest on his father's shoulders,
our daughter, toddling along the gravel road.
Our son finds a smooth stone, a trampled feather, a ber-
ried vine.
I gather cursed kudzu, surprised by grape-scented
blossoms.
Our daughter scoops chubby fistfuls of gravel,
clutching them home, its dust chalking her up to the
elbows.
She hoards her gravel like pirates' treasure.
We gather around the room,
each revealing a discovery:
a barbed loop of thorns, crown-size,
a swallow-shaped clay nest, empty as a tomb,
water clear and cold from the lake, scooped into a Sty-
rofoam cup,
a chambered hive, still sticky with honey.
She distracts and interrupts,
her baby prattle and calf-wobbly dance
an impromptu accompaniment to our worship.
She unclenches her burdened hands,
releasing handfuls of gravel onto the carpet,
a thousand voices of sound, its dust
sending up praise like incense.

BANANA BREAD

the chunk of banana bread
brown and crusty
until I bite into it
then the pale, moist flesh of it
thick with tiny black flecks of banana pulp
the taste of it
warm on my tongue
and the round smell of the molten butter
the ball of it soft in the back of my throat
peeling away of the last of my reserve
my skin becoming soft and
turning warm shades of ripe

9

MENTOR

When I was twelve, *A Wrinkle in Time* changed my life. Madeleine L'Engle's science-fiction novel took my mind, flipped it over, blew it up, bounced the pieces around, and shot them back into my head like rays of light, full of beauty and splendor and questions and possibilities. I responded by doing what any precocious kid would do: I wrote a letter to the author.

I told her that I loved her book and that it "made me think." I also asked about the book jacket's claim that she was "a practicing Christian." She wrote back, responding that she was glad the book made me think. She said the term "practicing Christian" wasn't hers, and that it unfortunately evoked images of hateful, judgmental behavior and ugly things like book burnings. She preferred to say that she was a believer who practiced every day at believing more, who tried to love others like God loved her, who valued good questions more than easy answers.

I was fascinated. I wasn't yet aware of the kind of ugly Christian she didn't like, but I knew instantly that I wanted to be the kind of Christian she was.

I continued to write Madeleine, and she continued to write me. I met her once, briefly, in high school, at a lecture she was giving in a nearby city. Then, in college, I went to the cathedral in uptown New York where I knew Madeleine had her office. In other words, I stalked her.

I asked the receptionist if Madeleine was in, and he said she'd be back soon. Ten minutes later, there she was, tall and fascinating — and a little intimidating. I introduced myself, and she recognized me immediately from our letters. We talked for an hour about science, God, and the discoveries that come with growing up. A few months later, while talking to one of her goddaughters, I found out that on the day of my visit, she had just heard that her husband of nearly forty years had cancer, and yet somehow she managed to make me feel welcome, listened to, important.

Three years later, my husband and I hosted her at a speaking event in our town. The following March, we stayed with her in New York in her spacious, rambling apartment full of books and art and an old Steinway. Her home testified to a life lived with love and generosity and beauty that I continue to try to emulate.

I saw her one more time. In the spring just before September 11th happened, Andrew, my son Lee, and I took her to lunch in the ground-floor restaurant of her Upper West Side apartment. Over lunch, I had the privilege of looking Madeleine in the eye and telling her — or trying to — exactly what she has meant to me. Her writing and thinking have become such a part of me that I hardly know, as my mother likes to put it, where my thinking starts and Madeleine's leaves off.

Knowing a famous author is worth nothing at all— or at least not any more than knowing a firefighter, a plumber, or a lawyer. But having a mentor saved and shaped my life.

●●●

In Madeleine's books about the Austin family, I found myself, my family, and my own questions of identity and self. I wrote to her again, saying that while I wished I was like the protagonist, Vicky, who was bookish, moody, and profound, I feared I was more like her little sister, Suzy, all sunshine and bubbles and simplicity, and did this make me shallow? Madeleine cautioned me not to judge Suzy, nor to think less of her because she was herself and not her sister. There is an important place for simplicity and joyfulness, and if I read the later books, I would discover Suzy all grown up and a well-respected doctor. In that exchange, Madeleine affirmed me to myself. In the ensuing difficult years of junior high and high school, she gave me the courage I would need both to be who I was and to allow myself to become who I am.

Over the years, the messages and ideas in Madeleine's books served to develop my own ideas and theology. Because of *A Wrinkle in Time*, I developed an interest in how science and faith become partners. After reading *Walking on Water*, I embraced and affirmed my calling as an artist. I learned to believe, like she did, that all "good" art is of God, because it is incarnational by nature and reflects the image of God in each of us. All "bad" art isn't art at all but only a poor imitation of this image. In her novels, I found myself, again and again, and as I grew, this image grew with me, sometimes nudging me forward into adulthood when I was hanging back, and sometimes pulling me back into my childhood when I was charging ahead too quickly.

I got word this week that Madeleine died. She was old, and in pain, so I know death was, in many ways, a blessing. But my heart has been breaking all week with grief and with gratitude. Grief, because in the face of disbelief, Madeleine was a light whose life said that faith is worth it, that we shouldn't be afraid of the hard questions, that we should continue to believe and create, because, as she said, "It is the nature of Love to create." I am grateful because she lived in my lifetime and shared part of herself with me, and because her writing and characters will always be with me and be part of who I am. I simply would not be who I am without her.

●●●

A mentor is not a parent. I have parents, and they fulfill their role in ways that continue to amaze and awe me. I didn't look for a mentor to replace my parents; I looked for a mentor who already lived the way I long to live. A mentor, by some miracle of grace, connects my present self with who I might become.

I read a book once on treating mothering and housekeeping as an art form and a ministry. The author sought out a group of older mothers who could counsel her; she called them her Committee. They had each been there and done that, and she consulted them when she was confused, bewildered, or in need of support.

I know a lovely couple — the man was my high school math teacher — who have successfully raised nine healthy, smart, and balanced children. They did it without pacifiers, disposable diapers, or formula, and while I didn't quite live up to all that, you can bet I called them for advice constantly.

I called, and still call, my own mother and father for advice on parenting, or to thank them for some particular habit they instilled in me or some skill they nurtured. I wouldn't want to try to get along without them, even now.

So when I say I need a mentor, I don't mean someone I can ask for advice. A mentor is a person who is not previously connected with me, who isn't required to love me, and who has perspective on life in general and on my life in particular. A mentor doesn't have anything to lose by telling me the truth. And a mentor sees me as a whole person, and not simply as a mother, a wife, an artist, or whatever. This person models wholeness in a fractured world and helps to lead me in the way I should go.

●●●

I met Ann at church. She and her husband, Nathan, were missionaries in Japan for about thirty years, and in Korea for five years. My mother's parents were pastors, and their table was usually filled with traveling evangelists and missionaries on furlough, as well as anyone who just needed a warm meal. Ann and Nathan were frequent visitors, and my mother often spoke admiringly of them.

After my third baby was born, I was praying in earnest for a mentor. One Sunday, while our church was searching for a pastor, Ann took a turn to preach. I have no recollection of what she said that day, but her spirit, peace, and charm captivated me. I waited nervously after the service for my turn to speak with her. Taking a deep breath, I jumped right in.

"I'd like to get to know you. I'd like you to get to know me. I need a mentor."

She put her hands on my shoulders and looked at me intently for a moment, her clear blue eyes sparkling. "You look like someone I'd like to know. You look like you're alive. When can we meet?"

I met Ann at church one morning every week while my two older kids were in preschool. I brought the baby with me. We talked about books we were reading and things we were thinking. We prayed. We laughed. She says I became her good friend. I say she became my "rabbi," my teacher. It wasn't until later that I understood just how many friends she had, and that at her age, to work another one into her already demanding schedule of speaking, traveling, teaching, and counseling was astounding. I'm grateful I had the audacity to come out and ask for her time.

Several years later, Nathan lost his twelve-year battle with cancer. His funeral overflowed with stories from people whose lives he and Ann changed for the better. Because of Nathan's health, neither he nor Ann had been back to Japan in many years, although they had many friends and memories there. Andrew and I had been saving air miles for years from our credit card, wondering what we would do with them. At Nathan's funeral, Andrew looked at me and said, "We're supposed to take Ann back to Japan."

A few months later, Andrew, my mother, our ten-year-old son, and I flew with Ann to Japan. We spent two magical weeks meeting her friends, visiting her sites, and sharing in her memories. We visited churches they started, met pastors and teachers they mentored, and toured cities they loved. In Osaka, we even met a young missionary who is teaching English at Sagwa University and following in Ann's footsteps. Everywhere we went, Ann led the way, pulling her small black suitcase behind her, speaking fluent Japanese to every surprised cab driver and train conductor, and usually calling back to us to stay together and keep up with her.

In Fukushima City, we met the family of four children, now grown, for whom Nathan and Ann built a house in their back yard when their father left them homeless. Neither Nathan nor Ann had any money, but they asked the US army base nearby for any discarded lumber they might have and built the entire house with it for these children, their mother, and their grandmother. Because of their gratitude to Ann and Nathan, those four people, with their spouses and children, hosted us at a beautiful mountain hot springs spa, fed us a twelve-course banquet, and led us on an incredible and exhausting one-day tour of their mountain resort region. To this day, these grown children love Ann so much they send her presents all year long and also to anyone she brings to meet them, us included.

In Kyoto, Ann took us to one of Nathan's favorite spots in all the world, a garden famous for its irises. Surrounded by irises of every color, we marveled at the beauty, then sat speechless beside Ann while she sat smiling at the sight, tears running down her face as she remembered the last time she was there with Nathan. We felt so privileged to be allowed to accompany her on this journey.

●●●

I called Ann this morning. She's been sick, and I wanted to check on her. If I'm honest, though, I also called because she never fails to pass along a wise insight. Today she told me she's been grappling with the "awesome power of choice" as God's biggest risk. She is astounded by His trust in us, and by the fact that we can't operate *without* making choices. She says this as she lies in bed, fighting a persistent infection that stops her with coughing fits every few sentences.

Last year she taught me that living with expectations is a sure way to end up disappointed, frustrated, and possibly bitter. But if we live each day with expectancy, we can't help but receive gifts. Her life seems to offer a constant "what's next, Papa?" to her loving God.

She once told me the story of a friend who wanted to be close to her and to Nathan, even though his doubts prevented him from having much in common with their worldview. He explained, "Your heart is so warm with the fire of love for God that it's enough for me right now to warm myself beside it." Perhaps in time his own fire would ignite, she said. It's not our job to defend God, she told me. It's to love people and *serve* God, allowing His contagious love to speak for itself.

Ann's wisdom has taught me so much about my children. If I approach them with expectations, we're all likely to be discouraged. But if I wake up each day and look at them with expectancy, they may surprise, delight, and please me in limitless ways. She inspires me with her continuous hunger for learning. She told me that she's meeting with a group of young mothers every month, and that one of them just taught her that when we don't teach our children how to fail, we teach them how to hide. Children who aren't allowed to fail feel that they must hide it when they do fail; they become dishonest about themselves and feel that they must perform in order to be loved. Instead, we should be teaching them how they can learn from failure, and that there is no failure that will separate them from God's or our love.

● ● ●

My oldest son is entering, in Eugene Peterson's words, that fascinating and scary laboratory that is adolescence. So far, he's pretty amazing. My prayers for him are changing, though. I am praying less for my own wisdom in parenting him and more that he will seek out wisdom on his own. I pray that he will seek out friends and mentors and authors that lead him into deeper questions and fuller love and who, like the great cloud of witnesses, will cheer him on, speaking from their experience of pain and joy and loss and healing. I pray that he will study Scripture and pray. Such things are the seeds of our growth in God, the shoots which become fruit-bearing branches when we plant ourselves near streams of living water.

One day, I pray, others will be drawn to the fruit and shade of his wide branches, just as I am drawn to Ann's.

THE NATURE OF LOVE

For Madeleine L'Engle, 1918–2007

Start with a poem,
she might have said.
All poems lead somewhere . . .
God knows you can't speak
the big things in prose —
just read the Bible.
The amoeba theory:
a creature with no skeletal structure —
free indeed —
but I doubt it has much fun.
It is the nature of Love to create.
Her thoughts fold into my own
like salt into the batter.
The desire to cry
for help is proof enough
we cry to something.
We are all connected;
the only independent
cells are cancer cells.
Redemption is to make us more
human, not less.
The real scandal is God
made man,
too radical for most of us.
Oh, friend, I still need you.
I'm grateful your silence
is so loud.

WAITING: LATE WINTER

A place to start is all I need,
one line that leads.
I will wait.
I sit still,
hoping for the rest to start,
for my heart to stop
its staccato tap and the breath
to begin its gentle dipping
in and out of the pool
at the bottom of my stomach.
I sip my coffee, inhaling its earthy steam,
listening to the cello,
weeping like a lost lover on the stereo.
The books stand like ready sentinels
on their shelves around me.
I am expectant.
The fog that froze its
hoary self to every branch and stem
has vanished like night, and the sun is sending
a watery, tentative light in through
the library blinds, falling
coolly on my legs, hinting
that there is more to come,
after the thaw, after the long winter.

10

BOOKS

I love clever people. I find clever people on pages of books. Sometimes they are characters, and other times they are the authors themselves, although I'm not sure I'd separate the two.

I think I have a reading problem. I carry only purses that have room for a book. I have two small bookcases in the kitchen — one for cookbooks, of course, and one for the current lineup. The lineup is the stack of books waiting on deck for me to read. It includes novels, memoirs, and classics. There are usually about seven or eight there at a time.

Let me explain: when I get up in the morning, I get the kids ready and off to school, and then I clean up the kitchen and fix my breakfast and coffee. That's when I sit down in my red chair by the fire — my mother had a chair by the fire in her kitchen, surrounded by stacks of books; I come by it honestly — and read whatever devotional I'm reading and the Bible and have some prayer time before the day takes off and I have to be on it.

A word here about devotionals: for the last couple

of years, when university is in session, my friend Eileen and I have been meeting once a week to discuss certain spiritual or devotional books. We are very picky about what we read. We give ourselves ever bigger and more ambitious assignments. This semester we will be reading some of the desert mothers, the female Christian mystics, as well as committing ourselves to reading and praying the daily offices, practiced by untold numbers of saints for centuries. We want to see what will happen.

When school isn't on, I read my own choice of devotionals. It might be anything from daily readings of C. S. Lewis or Dietrich Bonhoeffer or Frederick Buechner. I'm always working on a book from the Bible. Currently I'm reading daily readings from Madeleine L'Engle's writings, in honor of her life and death, and carefully chewing on Paul's letters to the churches. I'm always fascinated with the early church, hoping to catch a glimpse of what God intends for us.

If I'm home for the day, I'll usually read whatever novel or memoir I'm reading while I eat my lunch, a practice not recommended by diet experts, but it's one of the truly great pleasures of life, so what can you do? (When I was in college and living alone, I scheduled my classes so that I could be back in my little room for lunch. I'd sit at my desk with a big bowl of Special K with raisins and read a book not required by any of my classes. For a middle-child bookworm from a loud and busy family, this was pure heaven.)

If I'm out for the day, the book goes with me, in

case I have to wait in line at the bank or the doctor's office, or in case my friend is late in meeting me for lunch. If I'm driving, I'm listening to a book on tape, usually from the library. I am so thankful for this invention. What great, vast bits of time do we keep from wasting now that we can have someone read to us while we drive! I live in a small town, and it doesn't take very long to get anywhere, but you'd be surprised how many books I go through just running errands, picking up kids, waiting in line, and so forth. I prefer the books read by good actors, or sometimes by the authors themselves, especially if they have exceptional and intriguing voices, like Rick Bragg, or Frances Mayes, or Anne Lamott.

While I wait for my son to come out of middle school (and he always seems to be one of the last), I go through the day's mail and papers, which I pick up from the mailbox on the way out of the driveway. If Madeleine has dance class and it's my turn to drive, that's two and a half hours I have to wait, so I usually take any grading I have, along with any reading that needs to be done for class that week.

The late afternoons and evenings are reserved for homework help, cooking dinner, cleaning up dinner, lessons, and practices. After showers and baths, I get to read to Simon, my youngest. Although he is only five, he has recently declared a moratorium — I'm hoping it's just a hiatus — on picture books in favor of "chapter books" like the Junie B. Jones series. Currently we are reading *Peter Pan*. If I'm lucky, the older two will allow me to read aloud a book with them, something we are all interested in. Lee and I recently finished *Treasure Island*.

When they are all in bed, if I'm not too tired, I may get back to my book while I'm in the bath, or in bed until Andrew's ready to talk and be with me. If it's a really good book, I'll go to sleep thinking about it and wondering when I'll get a chance to read the next day.

So when I say I have a reading problem, I mean that my day is organized around reading. Units of time allotted for reading, and the specific material read in those units, give structure to my days. Each unit feels like a kiss from grace itself. It's no surprise, then, that when I have too many days that don't allow for any reading at all — and of course I do have those days — I begin to feel, well, a bit lost, unstructured, unread.

The kind of writing that gets me really going is writing that takes me from an easy and sure place to a new and pushy place of change and delight, challenge and awareness, discovery and beauty. I love it especially if it does this with some panache, pathos, poetry, or humor. I love emerging from a book as from a particularly satisfying and eye-opening dream, shaking myself off and realizing I'm not exactly the same person who started reading the book. I love discovering the people who inhabit the book, as though I've finally met the friends I've been looking for.

Some books, like some people, seem to have such potential for joy but end up disappointing or falling short in some way. Some books, like rare meals, not only fill you up but nourish you on some deep, cellular level, feeding your aesthetic and spiritual needs as well as your interest. Some books are more like a snack from the vending machine: satisfying for a short while, but not really sticking to your ribs. Some are like fast food, promising nourishment, but making you sluggish and hungry. Some, like candy, taste good going down and give you a short rush, but then leave you feeling empty and headachy.

The books I list here, in no particular order, are the rare meals.

I'm well aware that there are already so many good and true books written about the blessings of good and true books that it's a bit redundant, if not downright arrogant, for me to add my two cents to them. Madeleine L'Engle writes lovingly of several important books in her book *A Circle of Quiet* and about the importance of story in her book *The Rock That Is Higher: Story as Truth*. Eugene Peterson's book *Take and Read: Spiritual Reading; An Annotated List* left me so depressed after reading through it I thought I might have to quit reading altogether. I thought, What's the point? There is so much in print, all the classics that were written in the centuries and decades and years before I was born, and then all the bestsellers and pretty good books written since I was born, still being written ... I mean, why bother? I'll never make a dent. And Peterson seemed not only to have read all these books and digested them; he was able to comment intelligently on them — somehow while retranslating the entire Bible. I just thought, I give up. I did quit reading, actually. For about twenty-four hours. Then I needed something to read, to get my mind off it.

Anyway, I started keeping a journal of books I've read and any thoughts I have on them. And recently, I made a list of books that have saved my life. Without them, I think I would be lost. I think this is also known as a bibliography, or an annotated bibliography, as I will be audacious enough to add my thoughts and opinions about each book. But here I will just call it a list, and let you draw your own conclusions.

FICTION

All novels by Madeleine L'Engle, but specifically:

A Ring of Endless Light. I read this every summer for about seven years. It is for sentimental and other reasons my favorite book.

The Small Rain. This is Madeleine's first novel. It moves me every time I read it. It is about a young pianist named Katherine and her growth into herself as a woman and an artist. It lovingly explains the artistic temperament, especially to the artist herself.

The Love Letters. A very romantic and sexy novel based on the real letters of a Portuguese nun to the French soldier who seduced her and made her love him. A beautiful and honest picture of what it is like to try to integrate one's desire to please God with one's desires for human intimacy, and the part pride plays in the struggle.

The Other Side of the Sun. A wonderful and complex novel about a young English lady trying to adjust to life in the American South at the turn of the century. As in all of Madeleine's novels, evil is shown its way to the door through great love.

A Severed Wasp. The rich sequel to her first novel, written many years later. The heroine, Katherine, is now in her sixties, facing retirement, and finding that her struggles at this time in her life are not altogether different from when she was an adolescent, except that now she can draw on a lifetime of experience to help her navigate.

A Swiftly Tilting Planet. The most romantic of her science-fiction/fantasy, full of legends, memory, and hope.

A Prayer for Owen Meany by John Irving. This book quite simply astounds me in every way: characters, story, image . . . all the hallmarks of a great book.

The Starbridge novels of Susan Howatch. These novels I read and reread. They are the most amazing combination of dead-on theology, life-saving psychology, and page-turning plot I have ever found in a book. They teach me about healing and renew my belief that true wholeness through God's healing is not only possible but certain for those who seek it.

The books of L. M. Montgomery. Not only *Anne of Green Gables* but *Emily of New Moon* and the other clever and sensitive heroines of her books continue to inspire me, and other girls, especially now that I have a daughter.

Sense and Sensibility by Jane Austen. Of all of Austen's books, this one gives me the most faith in people and in true love, not to mention in old-fashioned good behavior.

Jane Eyre by Charlotte Bronte. I think of all the Bronte sisters, I'd like Charlotte the best. She seems so interesting without being brooding. Of all the Bronte novels, I love this one the most for its themes of loyalty, passion, and purity. What a fascinating family this must have been — all that illness and sadness and death, all that imagination, all the inner resources, all the creativity, all those howling moors. I am haunted by them.

Possession by A. S. Byatt. This is a contemporary masterpiece. It's also a literary thriller, which means that the detectives are actually academics, and the clues for which they are hunting are buried in books, letters, poetry, prose, and fiction. Not only has Byatt created characters and a plot that stop your heart, but she created *the entire body of written work* for the two literary figures. Mind-boggling. Very romantic too.

All books by E. M. Forrester. This is the man who gave us the books that became some of the most award-winning movies of our time: *Howard's End*, *Where Angels Fear to Tread*, *Passage to India*, *Maurice*, and my favorite, *A Room with a View*. One of my favorite passages in all of literature is in *Howard's End* (beginning of the fifth chapter). Helen hears Beethoven's Fifth Symphony in a music hall and *sees* it all as images in her head: goblins and elephants tromping on the globe and so forth. It explained me to myself, how I see music as images, and people as colors, and odd things like that. I also love this time period — Edwardian. I love the clothes from this period. You have to forgive me; I'm an actress.

All books by Edith Wharton, specifically:

The Age of Innocence. Again, I love this time period, but I especially love hearing about it from a woman's point of view. I love reading about our country, specifically New York, at this point in its development, before it was spoiled by industry and poverty and other byproducts of the industrial age. It also breaks my heart how the people in this book lose the courage for what it takes to be real, and to have real love.

Summer. A beautiful little novella, this is my favorite story of innocence lost and a young girl's coming of age.

The House of Mirth. Easily the saddest book I've ever read.

Jude the Obscure by Thomas Hardy. Tragic, rich, and compelling.

Far from the Madding Crowd by Thomas Hardy. My first experience with a really grown-up, classical piece of romantic literature. What a glorious introduction.

Memoirs of a Geisha by Arthur Golden. I've read this novel about three times now. I'm haunted by it.

It's what made me want to go to Japan. It also made me fascinated with the geisha world, although my Japanese friends can't figure out why.

The Secret Life of Bees by Sue Monk Kidd. This is a beautiful example of a terrific piece of contemporary fiction (I remind myself when I get snobbish about classic literature). I couldn't stop thinking about it long after I finished it. I've completely produced, cast, directed, and acted in the movie in my mind.

All books by Adriana Trigiani, especially:

> *Lucia, Lucia.* I read this in Italy and bawled my head off on the plane all the way home. It makes me long for a time I never knew, and so can't logically miss. But I miss it anyway.
>
> Big Stone Gap series. One part Virginia mountains hillbilly, and one part Italian countryside. Great characters, funny and sensitive writing, true love, and amazing food. What else do you need?

The Girl of the Limberlost by Gene Stratton Porter. Porter is one of the great writers for young people. She also happens to be from Indiana. I grew up on her books and love the naturalist/Cinderella aspects of her stories. She's wholesome and simple, both things I love about the Indiana countryside. She was also writing during my favorite time period.

All books by Elizabeth Peters. Everybody needs a little fluff, vacation reading, something fun and not too challenging. I prefer mine to be about interesting places, sporting intelligent and sassy heroines solving intelligent and sassy mysteries, written by intelligent and sassy authors with PhDs in Egyptology.

The Color Purple by Alice Walker. When Andrew and I were dating, we had to be apart all summer, so we gave each other our four most important books to read. That way we could still be getting to know each other while we were apart. This was one of his. I loved the book, and I see my husband all over it, and love him more for loving it. This book gets to the heart of women in a way that few books — or men — have the courage to do.

Chasing Francis by Ian Morgan Cron. A novel by the pastor of a megachurch, about a pastor of a megachurch, who has what he assumes is a crisis of faith — fortunately or unfortunately — in front of his congregation. What it turns out to be, though, is a crisis of tradition, which is actually a good thing to have now and then, especially when it leads you on a pilgrimage to Italy and a discovery of ancient truths that end up informing your future.

Quite a Year for Plums by Bailey White. A quirky novel about quirky people in a small Southern town — is that redundant? — who weave in and out of each other's experiences with charming insight and gentle humor. I love these people, and I love Bailey White's voice reading the audio book. (She's a regular on NPR.) If I had more money, I'd buy the option on this book and produce the movie. I've got it all cast in my head. It wouldn't be a blockbuster, but I know some people who would enjoy it.

All books by Diane Mott Davidson. My husband loves the Food Channel because he loves food. I love food too, but with a little murder mystery thrown in — hence, my affection for Davidson's books. The heroine's an Episcopalian caterer married to a detective and living in a beautiful small resort town in Colorado. Something about the whole setup rings strangely true. She has an evil and powerful ex-husband and a bright and awkward teenage son, and when she is troubled or puzzled, she cooks. In the printed versions, you get the recipes. The talented and witty Cherry Jones reads many of the audio books.

The plays of Shakespeare. Even though I am an actor and an acting teacher, I don't like to read plays, least of all Shakespeare's plays. I hold this is because plays weren't written to be read; they were written to be performed — especially Shakespeare. On the other hand, of all the plays I love to work on, study, direct, act, and chew on, Shakespeare's quite easily take the cake. I quote the updated movie version of *Taming of the Shrew* called *Ten Things I Hate about You*: "I don't just *like* Shakespeare; we're *involved.*" There are no words that taste better than Shakespeare's. I have a collection of his anthologies. If my house were burning, I'd get the kids out, then the dogs, then I'd grab my Riverside Edition of *The Complete Works of William Shakespeare*.

The Education of Little Tree by Forrest Carter. The impact this book had on me was like a knife in the chest. I also remember there was some scandal about this not being a true story, as originally thought, but I didn't care. Whether it is fact or not, it is still true.

Christy by Catherine Marshall. When I read this book, I was in great need of an explanation for the suffering in the world. This story does a particularly beautiful and poignant job of doing just that. It also marked the beginning of my fascination with and love for Appalachia.

A Tree Grows in Brooklyn by Betty Smith. A truly beautiful novel about life in the poverty classes of Brooklyn in the first decades of the twentieth century. Gorgeous and moving.

SPIRITUAL/THEOLOGY

All books by Madeleine L'Engle, but specifically:

Walking on Water. Singer/songwriter Nichole Nordeman says, and rightly so, that this should be required reading for every artist. My mother assumes that it *is.*

A Circle of Quiet. A fascinating and tender glimpse into Madeleine's thinking, struggles, family life, work, and faith.

Laughter in the Walls by Bob Benson. I grew up knowing Bob Benson and his family. I grew up hearing these beautiful and elegant prose poems read at dinner, for audiences at concerts, and in small, intimate worship gatherings. I return to them again and again and use them when I lead worship.

All books by Robert Benson, but specifically:

Living Prayer. Although I've known Robert all my
life (he's one of Bob Benson's sons), this book
was my introduction to his writing. It exqui-
sitely knits the stuff of our days into a prayer
that we wear like a shawl as we go about our
business. It was the book that caused me to call
my mother and my sister and exclaim breathlessly, "He's like Bob Benson . . . only better!"
The chapter on planting sweet peas is particularly breathtaking.

Digging In. In this book Robert details how he
and his family created a garden paradise in his
back yard with hard labor, sweat, planning,
and other people's castoffs. In the process,
he finds both hilarity and holiness. As a gar-
dener, I couldn't have been more enthralled. As
a writer, I couldn't have been more sure that I
wanted to be Robert Benson when I grew up.

Venite. A prayer book that Robert put together
as he was himself discovering how to pray. I
return to it when I feel I need to restitch the
fraying seams of my discipline.

Waking the Dead by John Eldridge. We just finished studying this book in house church. It's by far
one of the most important books I've ever read. It
should be required reading for anyone serious about
living an empowered and fully awake life.

Traveling Mercies by Anne Lamott. For anyone
interested in the sheer variety of ways God chooses to

pursue people. Lamott is undisputedly a great writer (and a wonderful speaker, if you ever get a chance to hear her, but don't bother if you're easily shocked or believe that all real Christians talk, act, or think the same way). She's sharp, vulnerable, honest, a little crazy, and deadly funny. She's wrestled way too many demons to the ground to lie about it. I love her.

Disciplines for the Inner Life by Bob and Michael Benson. Michael is another one of Bob's sons. I return to this book every couple of years. It's chock full of a broad scope of writings by saints, theologians, and sojourners. It's set up for daily spiritual discipline, but it goes far beyond a simple "quiet time." Each day, you read and meditate on psalms, hymns, Scripture, prayers, and readings, all set up in weekly themes. It's a treasure.

Wishful Thinking: A Theological ABC by Frederick Buechner. This is a great reference book for theological and spiritual questions. It's set up like a glossary, so when I'm grappling with a concept and get into a muddle, I like to look up how Buechner defines it. His wisdom, clarity, and levity tend to wash the crud off my thinking and let the sunlight back in. I especially love his discussions of the terms *atheist, doubt, lust,* and *theology.*

So the Woman Went Her Way by Lynne Bundesen. This book came to me at an important time in my life, when I was in graduate school and trying to reconcile my feminist sensibilities with how I should live my life as a Christian. By telling the story of her journey,

Bundesen leaves me no doubt as to how Jesus felt about women, and about my place in His heart.

Blue Like Jazz by Donald Miller. I'm sure everyone's read this book by now. It came out of the Christian publishing world like a blazing comet, aiming at the postmodern generation, but showering light, humor, and truth on many others along the way. It did everything a good book is supposed to do; it grabbed me, held me, made me laugh out loud, moved me, challenged me, and forced me to buy ten copies to give to all my friends.

Searching for God Knows What by Donald Miller. This is deeper and more profound than *Blue Like Jazz* and does a really beautiful job of picking up the beginning of the thread in the garden of Eden and feeling along it through Calvary and all the way to us here in the twenty-first century. It still reflects Miller's humor and sense of discovery, but is much more grounded in his maturity as a disciple of Jesus. If *Jazz* is the story of Miller's birth in Christ, *Searching* is his bar mitzvah.

Secrets of the Vine by Bruce Wilkinson. Most people know Wilkinson through his famous book *The Prayer of Jabez*, but I found this little gem more illuminating and profound. It's one of those discoveries that made me say, "Oh ... of *course*! It's so simple! Why didn't I understand that before?"

Sabbath Keeping by Donna Schaper. For Christmas one year I made "Sabbath baskets" for all of my family, with this book in it along with tea, bubble bath, and other aids for rest. I love this little book for using

Sabbath as a verb, and for getting to the root of why Sabbath is such a loving gift, made for our health and joy, from our Father.

The Message by Eugene Peterson. This is often referred to as a paraphrase of the Bible. From what I understand of Peterson's process, though, it may be more accurate to call it a prayerful translation from the original languages, *not* from later and less faithful translations like the Vulgate. However he did it, it is pretty clear Peterson deeply loves the Scriptures and the God to whom they point. It isn't an exaggeration to say that reading and hearing the Scriptures from this version has often been life-changing. It so often helps to hear things with a fresh ear. I am grateful to Eugene Peterson for this painstaking and poetic work of love. I also appreciate his introductions to each book, which distill the thrust of the book so well into clear little nuggets.

Reclaiming God's Original Intent for the Church by Wes Roberts. This book messed with me enough to make me ask some really hard questions about what I thought church is, which led to some really hard decisions about how we do church. It made me ask myself the necessary but painful question, What exactly is it that I am going to church to worship?

Experiencing God by Henry Blackaby. I recommend this study to people who are on the brink of making big choices or making profound changes in their lives — or sometimes if they are just bored and stymied. Be ready, though, I warn them. If you really are ready for God to rearrange your head, He will. It may rock your world. It did mine, and I am so grateful.

NONFICTION

The books of Frances Mayes. What can I say? I'm a sucker for sumptuous writing about sumptuous food in sumptuous places. I can only say I am thankful that Ms. Mayes cut her teeth, so to speak, writing for food and travel magazines. I am richer for it.

All books by Bill Bryson, specifically:

> *Notes from a Small Island.* Not your average travel journal. Bryson is split-your-sides funny, and wickedly perceptive. My husband hasn't actually read these books, but he may as well have, since I read so much of them aloud to him. This one is about a hiking tour of the UK Bryson made before moving back to America after living in England for twenty-five years.
>
> *Neither Here nor There.* This is the account of Bryson's trip during college across Europe with his sometimes-buddy Katz. Again, not your average travel book. Hilarious. This is the book that made me decide, "I'll pretty much read anything he writes."
>
> *A Walk in the Woods.* Okay, so it's clear I like funny books. This one is about hiking the Appalachian Trail. I laughed so hard I ... well, never mind, but I also learned a lot about hiking, Appalachia, eastern America, and bears.

84 Charing Cross Road by Helene Hanff. Funny, tender, clever letters to an old friend made through correspondence over — what else? — books. It's really a love letter to books themselves. Also a really great movie with Anne Bancroft and Anthony Hopkins. Legend has it Bancroft loved the book so much her husband, Mel Brooks, bought her the movie rights for her birthday and produced it for her to star in. Pretty great present, huh?

A Girl Named Zippy by Haven Kimmel. My favorite memoir. All the more favorite because all of the events described in this book happened in exactly my era (the author is my age) about twenty-five minutes from where I grew up (Moorland, Indiana). Hilarious, precarious, and alarmingly sharp.

She Got Up off the Couch by Haven Kimmel. A continuation of *A Girl Named Zippy*, this time focusing on Kimmel's astounding couch-potato mother. A real caterpillar-into-a-butterfly story.

Cheaper by the Dozen by Frank B. Gilbreth and Ernestine Gilbreth Carey. Great fun and a huge inspiration for creative parenting. Unlike the movie with Steve Martin, the original family lived in the 1920s, which makes their choices and lifestyles (both parents were professionals as well as full-time parents of — yep — *twelve* biological children) even more astonishing.

If You Want to Write by Brenda Ueland. Frank talk on good writing. I read it twenty-some years ago and am only just beginning to apply it.

The Writing Life by Annie Dillard. A short and inspiring book on Dillard's writing practices, although she can't write anything practical for very long without it morphing into stunning philosophy and theology. I often feel I'm not even worthy of reading her, but I read her anyway.

Holy the Firm by Annie Dillard. Ditto. Writing that is really and truly great art. Take off your shoes.

Ava's Man by Rick Bragg. Bragg is a Pulitzer Prize–winning journalist for the *New York Times*. He comes from the dirt-poor hills of Appalachia, and his story is both typical and astonishingly unusual. His writing is pure, like glass, or water. This is the story of his grandfather, whom he never knew, except through stories. This is the only book that, when my husband finished listening to the audio book (Bragg reads it), he took out the last cassette and put the first one in again to start over. I recommend the audio book; Bragg's voice is so heartbreakingly beautiful, you will fall in love with him.

All Over but the Shoutin' by Rick Bragg. This is Bragg's first book. In it, he tells both his own story and the story of the woman who made his possible: his remarkable mother. His prose is poetry with teeth.

All books by Thomas Cahill, but especially:

> *How the Irish Saved Civilization.* A fascinating glimpse into Celtic Christianity and how it may have kept the light from going out completely in the Dark Ages.
>
> *The Gifts of the Jews.* A careful and loving look at

what we think we know about Judeo-Christian society and thought, and how that impact benefits us more than we may realize.

The Desire of the Everlasting Hills. A compelling historical and sociological investigation of the birthplace and time of Jesus Christ. Why then? Why there? As it turns out, it may be more a miracle of a historical nature than just a theological one.

Mysteries of the Middle Ages. With great relish, Cahill looks at major figures in the Middle Ages, such as Dante, Thomas Aquinas, Giotto, and my favorites, Hildegard of Bingin and the tragic lovers Heloise and Abelard. (As Cahill says, Romeo and Juliet have nothing on these two. Talk about passion!)

A note on Cahill: I understand most academic historians find Cahill a bit of a lightweight. He may be. I'm not a historian. But I can tell you, I find reading straight historical theory as much of a bore as the next guy. Cahill brings history to life for me, and I've learned more about the loves, losses, tragedies, and triumphs of humanity reading his books than in all the history classes I ever took put together. He has a passion for humanity and what its past can teach us that is altogether contagious.

Mama Makes Up Her Mind by Bailey White. Quite simply the best and funniest book of humorous essays I've ever read. White writes about everything from having an eye-to-eye encounter with a giant raptor bird, to the roaring alligator that lives in her back yard.

Holding Onto the Air by Suzanne Farrell. I'm a bit obsessed with George Balanchine and his brainchild, the New York City Ballet. Farrell, his beautiful protégé and "muse," writes a lovely and moving account of her development as one of the greatest ballerinas of all time, and of her fascinating relationship with the man who helped create her. (When I get to heaven, I will dance like Suzanne Farrell. And sing like Alison Krauss — but that's another story.)

A Winter's Season: A Dancer's Journal by Toni Bentley. Bentley was a company member of the aforementioned NYCB. This is her journal from a year during which she came to grips with being a permanent member of the corps, never being able to advance to principal, and finding joy in serving her art as a supporting player. She also talks a lot about loving Farrell, both as a dancer and as a person. It's a beautiful little book, as much about being an artist as it is about learning joy through humility.

Eat Pray Love by Elizabeth Gilbert. I just finished this book. I can't stop thinking about it. I would say it has changed how I think. I can't get over how very fundamentally *other* her path to God is from mine, and yet how much truth I came across in her story that resonated with my own understanding of God. She's raw and vulnerable, and honest and warty. Plus it's a travel book. Plus it's about good food. Plus she meets really fascinating people. Plus she's funny, funny, funny. I'm pretty sure she and I would be good friends, given the chance.

POETRY

The poetry of Mary Oliver, especially *Thirst*. This is the first book of poetry I ever read cover-to-cover, in order. Oliver's poetry looks so simple. But what Mary Oliver does is the absolute essence of poetry. And it's really, really difficult to do. After I read this book, I had to write a poem about reading her poetry. Maybe I'll send it to her. Or maybe I'll just keep reading her, hoping I can catch a glimpse of how she does what she does. She moves me so deeply, apparently without breaking a sweat.

The poetry of e. e. cummings. I wrote my independent study on cummings in college. No one writes love poetry better. He somehow flicks his wrist and comes out with poems that are inventive and pithy without being coy. He's a great example of how one has to learn the rules before one can break them with any authority. He's an original, but he expresses *my* soul so well. I had this stanza painted around our great room: "i thank You God for most this amazing / day: for the leaping greenly spirits of trees / and a blue true dream of sky; and for everything / which is natural which is infinite which is yes." Yes.

EXCAVATION

Look here,
This layer has all of humanity in it:
The words of all the poets
And how they knew about love
Passion jealousy laughter.
How they knew we'd need them
All this time later,
We'll never know,
But here they are.
I hear the declamation from the top of the theater.
I speak the words and
Still they echo
Centuries, no,
Millennia later.
And this stratus—
I doubt you'll notice the holes, the way
The marble lay on the ground too long
And began to take on the quality
Of water, of wood—
Became porous and lost its resilience.
This is the layer that we lost and
Though we know it existed,
We can't hear its words anymore.
Our loss,
Since I think it probably contained
Some piece, some morsel
Of truth or at least
Some feeling we might need now.

I know this:
I am an archeologist of time
Of words of
Poetry.
I dig for all of us.

READING MARY OLIVER

(first poem of the year)

Does she write them with her hand
around a pencil, on real paper,
or a black felt tip on a yellow legal pad?

Is she close to the poems
like the woods she has visited every day
for twenty years and the deer

who actually nuzzled her hand,
so like a poem she had to write one about it?
Maybe her computer is in a dark

room of her house, where the glowing screen
sends off light, illuminating
the room with her words

maybe there is an old black typewriter
that waits for her on her kitchen table:
when she returns from her walk, she

rolls in a sheet of white paper and
clicks it into place.
I don't know her.

I just know her poems, her walks,
her woods full of creatures and glimpses
of God: the pine needle, the rose, her own voice.

I can only imagine how she spins out
the words into poems, woven words
I use to cover myself during the cold

weeks of winter, or to cover my head like
a prayer shawl, as she ushers me into the temple,
where I kneel in holy worship.

11

MUSIC

When I was a child, music filled my house.

That sounds lovely, doesn't it?

Actually, it was cacophony.

There are five of us in my immediate family, and each of us had his or her own favorite style of music. My dad listened to southern gospel and black gospel. The Statesmen and Andraé Crouch and the Richard Smallwood Singers were balm to his soul.

My older sister loved R&B and good electric bass players; she even married one when she discovered he could play the "Stomp" bass solo. Her bands were Earth, Wind and Fire, the Silvers, Toto, and the Pointer Sisters.

My brother was a rocker. He carried around Ray Stevens and Neil Diamond albums when he was almost too small to hold the album covers under his little arms. He loved good hard rock bands: Van Halen, Bon Jovi, Journey, and Boston. Those aren't bands you listen to quietly, and he didn't.

If my mother ever got the chance to put on any of her music, it was likely to be instrumental or gentle singer/songwriters from the 1960s like Joan Baez or Judy Collins.

I discovered Broadway when I was in elementary school, and the only sounds that could compete with cast recordings from *Guys and Dolls* or *Annie* were the dancing strains of Tchaikovsky or the aching preludes of Chopin.

With so many sound waves competing for attention in our house, I used to shut myself in my room, tune my radio to the local classical station, and lie on my bed dreaming or reading. It felt like the only time I had to myself, to be who I really was.

● ● ●

I was in Paris the first time that I felt like a piece of music was created specifically for me. I was eleven, and we were traveling to Israel. A friend handed me her Sony Walkman, put the headphones over my head, and pressed the play button.

Tchaikovsky's "Waltz of the Flowers" from *The Nutcracker Suite* exploded into me. I was holding onto a wheeled baggage cart, and I pushed off across the smooth floor as if I were flying. I was clay, and the intricate fingers of Tchaikovsky's score were shaping me into something wholly different from and yet more myself than I had ever been before.

I had been waiting for that moment since before I was born. When my mother was singing in concerts and pregnant with me, she used to pray the audience wouldn't see her dress jumping as I kicked and danced inside her. I guess I have always had a visceral response to music.

I don't know when I became aware of music, but I know it has shone through every facet of my life. Even during moments of silence, music has been *there*, like a parent or air or God. Music is a necessity, a given. Music is omnipresent, like God — not because it is God, and not because we worship it, but because the one we worship is singing His song into our lives.

●●●

My mother is a child, five or six. She turns the corner between the kitchen and the parlor, her fingers tracing the wallpaper. She stops. Her father is sitting in his chair, his big, soft Bible open in his lap. He doesn't see her. Tears roll down his face as he reads the Word. Sudden understanding shines through my mother's fear: he is in love. The Word moves him beyond words. As her father cries, she knows this is true as surely as she knows the texture of the paper beneath her fingers: God is personal, and He stirs the passions of our hearts.

Years later another child walks into a room that is bursting with music. Her bare feet feel the vibrations of it through the floor. As the sound pours over her, she sees her father sitting on the stool by the record player. His head is tilted back, his teeth are bared by raw emotion, and tears pour out of eyes shut tightly. One hand is suspended in the air. Sudden understanding floods her ears, washing away her fear. The swelling, unresolved harmonies of a black choir strike an ache deep inside her she has never felt. As the chord resolves, her father's hand cuts slowly through the air on the final downbeat. His shoulders relax as a long-held breath is exhaled. She tiptoes out.

There are no words. There is only the music, even in the silence, its truth moving beyond words, beating to the rhythm of Love.

●●●

Many nights I went to sleep listening to my parents in the living room. Dad was at the piano, and Mom was sitting in a chair beside him, her yellow legal pad in hand. Dad might repeat the same line over and over on the keys; Mom might interrupt or hush him; they might argue; but before they went to bed, a new song would be echoing through the room.

My brother wrote his first song when he was three, a bouncy jingle with lyrics that went like this:

I went all the way
To the Kokomo Mall
With a hole in the seat of my pants!

When he was five, he wrote a full song, complete with two verses, a chorus, a bridge, and chords my sister could play on the autoharp while she sang backup vocals and he sang into a drumstick.

It is impossible to conceive of a family picnic, cookout, or vacation without the sound of guitars and singing. When she was thirteen, my sister spent her own money to have one of her songs made into a stu-

dio demo. Most of my family makes its living in the
music business, and most of the people in my parents'
lives, with the exception of some family members and
folks from our hometown where my dad grew up, had
something to do with music or its industry. We vacationed with some of them, traveled with them on the
weekends, and visited with them.

One of these people was Bob MacKenzie, my parents' producer. He was a small man, full of explosive
energy, a risk-taker who didn't wait to see how his
sometimes reckless enthusiasm would affect anyone
else. To me, he was magical, and a little frightening.
He and his wife, Joy, were like extra parents to me, and
their kids were some of my closest friends. I looked up
to the MacKenzies and hoped for their approval. I
remember one night being awakened at their house to
sing on a kids' project my parents were recording.

● ● ●

*The little girl sleeps peacefully in the trundle bed in
Shana's room. It is nighttime. The house was quiet earlier when she went to bed; her parents were in the studio
working on a children's album, and she was left with Joy
and the two girls. She does not hear the voices in the hall
now, whispering and arguing:*

"Absolutely not," she does not hear her mother say.

"Gloria," Bill reasons, "we've only got tonight."

"We'll have to come back then." She sounds firm.

*"No, no ... that's crazy," Bob interjects. "Let's get
it done tonight. No use coming back."*

"Bob . . ." *Gloria is getting angry.* "We're not waking her. She's six years old. It's nearly eleven."

"Oh," —*Bob is used to overriding protective mothers*— "she'll think it's an adventure. I'll do it."

Gloria shoots out an arm and stops him.

"No," *she says under her breath.* "I'll get her."

A half hour later, the little girl stands on the wood floor in her bare feet and yellow nightgown in front of a microphone. She wears headphones and is still blinking in the bright light of the studio.

Through the headphones she hears Bob's energetic voice. She strains to please him— *to please them all behind the glare of the control-room glass.*

"One more time, Amy. You've got a better one in you."

"Just one more, honey," *her mother's voice breaks in,* "then you can go back to bed."

"You don't want to go back to bed, do ya, Aims? Isn't this fun?"

She grins sleepily. Her head spins with excitement and drowsiness.

"Yeah. This is fun."

"Let's roll it, then!"

The piano sounds in her ear. She takes a breath.

"I am a pwwo-mise. I am a poss-i-bi-li-ty. I am a pwwo-mise. With a cap-i-tal P. I can be any-thiiing. Anything God wants me to beeeee."

The tape grinds to a halt.

"That's it! I think we got it. Come in and listen, Aimers!"

She takes off the phones and heads into the darkness of the booth, crawling up into her mother's lap. They listen. Her voice sounds funny to her, but they all seem pleased. Her mother squeezes her, and her daddy grins.

"That's sweet, honey. That's good."

She looks at Bob, whose fists are doubled up in enthusiasm. He shakes them in the air and laughs. This is a man I want as a fan, she thinks. He waltzes over to her and takes her face in his hands, kissing her carefully on the head.

"Brilliant, Aimers. Brilliant."

She glows.

It is a long time that night before she is able to sleep.

● ● ●

It is still these people, these music people, whom I want as fans. They still flavor me, like a tea bag changes the water it's steeped in. I still get excited when I get to see one of them; even as they age, they are the epitome of magic and adventure and, well, *music* that they were when I was a child.

● ● ●

We are driving. My father sing-talks to me, his voice a warm baritone.

"This is one."

I sit in the back seat, repeating the tone.

"One."

"Now, give me three."

My mind scrambles to climb the musical steps. My

pitch is not perfect, but I find the note with mental reasoning, unwilling to let him hear me do the figuring.

"Three," I sing.

He knows how I find it. It doesn't matter. The game has started, and we both enjoy it.

"Now, give me two."

Back to one, I think, then mentally, "One" — aloud, "Two."

We play like this: he tests; I challenge myself to do my mental gymnastics more quickly.

He falls silent, and I know he is thinking about — what? The days when he was a boy at the Stamps School, first learning intervals and harmonies? Or is he hearing the harmonies themselves? He fades farther away, and I think I can hear the echo of a scratchy 78 playing in his brain, sounds drifting down from upstairs at my grandma and grandpa's farmhouse.

I often fall asleep to those sounds, harmonies fading and blaring as singers with names like Denver Crumpler, Hovie Lister, and Jake Hess croon "The Bible Tells Me So" and "Happy Rhythm."

I know he is hearing them now, here, in the car. I watch him in the rearview mirror.

Nights when we have dinner guests, my father says, as the candles burn low, "Hey, can I play you something? Come in here." Long after I am supposed to be in bed, I sit at the top of the stairs in my nightgown, peering around the banister. My father's face dances with admiration, joy, astonishment, laughter, and tears. Our guests catch his fever: black gospel choirs, Andraé

Crouch, Richard Smallwood, Larry Gatlin and the
Gatlin Brothers. Even as I'm standing at the top of the
stairs, the harmonies make my heart ache.

"Daddy." I repeat it. "Daddy. Daddy."

"What?" He is still gone.

"Earth to Bill," my mother says.

He blinks, focuses. "What?"

"This is one," I say. Back to one.

He grins, returning. "Okay, give me seven." His
favorite interval.

Harmony is his home base, his root, his "one."

He plants me there, there in soil rich enough for
deep, deep roots.

"This is one."

I wait for the next call, resting for now on this refer-
ence point. We always come back to one.

● ● ●

Handel's *Water Music* was my first favorite classical piece. My cousin Melody introduced me to it when
I was eleven and she was twenty. Her choice of music
seemed to me the height of sophisticated joy. When
the leaves are falling off the trees and I am beginning
to think about what I am going to fix for our Thanksgiving feast, Handel's *Water Music* always enters my
spirit and flows from my speakers.

I first heard Barber's *Adagio for Strings* on my first
date with my husband. It builds a lofty and impos-
sibly fragile tower of longing and desire and sadness
and beauty. It was Andrew's first gift to me, and I will

always associate it with our discovery of each other in a world both heartbroken and hopeful.

Copeland's *Appalachian Spring* is a musical painting. One rainy day in early spring, I was driving with my tired and cranky kids when the public radio station began playing it. I turned up the volume and described to them the images I saw in my mind. Before long, the children were rapt, imagining crocuses pushing their hopeful buds through the snow-spotted earth; they heard the birds, just returned from their southern sojourn, trilling sweetly in the crisp morning air; they saw the breath of the fawn as she nuzzled closer to her mother's flank; they saw the sunrise spread like marmalade across the sky behind the mountain.

As the voice of the final clarinet faded, we sat quietly, our breathing slowing. My daughter broke the silence.

"Play it again, Mommy. I want to see it again."

This is the movement of music in our hearts and minds. We listen; we wait; we listen again.

●●●

I don't listen to music, I *see* it. Colors. Images. Characters. Scientists call me a sentient; they say I am synesthetic.

I call myself blessed.

●●●

My mother says that music is often how people can hear truth when other paths are closed — sort of a new way in. Music enters the brain differently than what we hear and read, and so it sneaks around the part of the brain that responds to reason and rationale alone.

I'm glad our brains have this safety valve that allows mystery and beauty, paradox and joy, art and wonder. Alzheimer patients, long after losing information like people's names and dates and facts, can sing songs word for word, and melody is one of the last things to go. In spite of what age and illness do to our bodies and brains, music is the open space wide enough to hold us all.

Vern, our friend from house church, struggles with names and conversation when we visit him — until we begin to sing. He not only remembers the words; he can still sing the tenor part. The songs lead us into the open spaces; music is a new way in.

● ● ●

Donna Schaper says that music, for many people, is the ladder to God. We all have our ladders. Silence is good too, but sometimes we need a window opened, a hole cut in the ceiling, and a way to climb into the light, or a way for the light to shine down into our darkness.

Perhaps that's why it was important for me to discover what *my* music is. At the center of a musical storm, I needed to be able to hear the sound of my footsteps on the ladder. "God has given me a new song," Scripture says, and I strain to catch the notes that He sings for my ear only.

I needed to pull away from all those wonderful

sounds — my dad's southern and black gospels; my sister's soulful R&B; my mother's wise and thoughtful folk singers; the energy of my brother's driving rock bands — so I could pick out my own tune: the emotion of Broadway, the romance of classical and ballet music, the haunting mystery of New Age and Celtic, the soulful harmony of bluegrass and mountain music, and a little bit of my own sound that bends them all into something that speaks specifically to me.

Maybe God called me away, like the lover in Solomon's garden, so He could build His own ladder to *my* window. He climbs to me, like Rapunzel's prince, and sings His love into my heart. He's always looking for a new way in.

THE MUSIC IN HER HEAD

Hear this, Mama,
she says, putting unplugged
earphones on my head.
Hear it, hear it—
the music in my 'magination's
'mazing—hear it!
I listen to the song
of her mind, tuning
to the sweet, faint
sounds of everything.

SINGING ALTO

sitting next to my mother
singing number three hundred fifty nine
—I Am the Lord's I Know—
a smooth third beneath the melody line
her deep voice a sonorous vibration
against my ear
—Whether I Live or Die—
—Whether I Wake or Sleep—
learning the alto line was not so
much a choice as this is how you sing
a hymn if you are a woman
in a church full of men, full of
ladies singing high, clear, right on the
obvious melody, full of basses
and baritones and tenors
but if you are different
if you understand that your part is to
give the melody something to lean on
if you understand that not everyone gets the spotlight
but without you, the song is thin and frail
if you understand that your value is in your belonging,
        your
place in this family, your being loved, your belovedness
not in singing high, singing loud, singing the main part
if you understand this
then maybe, maybe you too, can learn
the alto, a third below, smooth and sonorous enough
for a child to sleep comfortably, lulled to sleep by the
        vibration
the sound of belovedness

12

BELIEF

My friend Eileen and I are reading Sam Harris's *Letters to a Christian Nation*. Sam Harris is an atheist, and I suppose I'd be one too, but—like the old cliché goes—I don't have that much faith. It's a hard book to read. Debate isn't my strong point and arguing gives me a stomachache. But it's a good book to read—necessary, even—because belief and unbelief are rarely strangers.

Harris makes several valid points—statistics about the percentage of believers versus nonbelievers, and horrible facts about atrocities done in the world in the name of religion—which make me wonder why I still believe. Am I just stubborn, hanging onto my faith because it's comfortable? Or naïve? Are some people predisposed to belief, and we're either born believers or not?

Or does the problem boil down to bad marketing? I wouldn't believe in the god some churches preach either. Maybe it's a question, as Mark Lowry once said, of *which* god you don't believe in.

●●●

Above my desk is pinned this anonymous quote: "God must be very great to have created a world which carries so many arguments against his existence." Madeleine L'Engle writes that she has gone through periods "of agnosticism and even atheism." However, "[I] cannot live for long in this dead-end world, but return to the more open places of my child's intuitive love of God, where I know that all creatures are the concern of the God who created the galaxies, and who nevertheless notes the fall of each sparrow" (*A Circle of Quiet*).

My friend and mentor Ann says when she gets confused or feels lost, not sure where she is with God, she always comes back to two irrefutable truths that her long life has taught her: God is, and God cares. She can doubt and disbelieve—and has—almost every other tenet of the faith save these two. She finds she cannot live, as Madeleine says, without them for long.

I can't bring myself to believe this is because either Ann or Madeleine is weak or stubborn. Rather, I suspect they are wise in a way that looks like foolishness to unbelievers—and even, sometimes, to believers.

●●●

Many years ago my parents wrote a song called "I Believe, Help Thou My Unbelief." The title comes from the Scripture passage about the father of a sick child who asked Jesus to heal his son. It is one of the more endearing accounts of honesty in the Gospels; this father blurts out whatever will get him results and then, faced with the piercing gaze of Jesus, begs for help. "Of *course* I believe! Well, okay, maybe I don't always believe, but if You are God, You can help me with that too!"

Recently my dad grieved the loss of his longtime mentor, Robert Reardon. He was a man of God, a minister, and the president of Anderson University, a respected Christian college. He said once, "I believe. Most of the time. And that's pretty good." His death has brought my parents' song to mind, its melody planting deep roots in my soul.

> *I believe. Help Thou my unbelief.*
> *I walk into the unknown,*
> *Trusting all the while.*
> *I believe. Help Thou my unbelief.*
> *I walk into the unknown,*
> *Trusting like a child.*
> *I long so much*
> *To feel the warmth*
> *That others seem to know,*
> *But should I never feel a thing*
> *I claim Him, even so.*
> *I believe. Help Thou my unbelief.*
> *I walk into the unknown,*
> *Trusting . . .*

Mystery is reality. Car headlights illuminate only the road directly in front of me, a limitation that doesn't prevent me from driving all the way home. I am becoming more and more comfortable with my lack of certainty and vision, which means I'm becoming either lazier or more childlike.

● ● ●

My mother has a hard time getting trivial facts straight. *A River Runs Through It* becomes *A Creek down the Middle*. *Something's Gotta Give* becomes *It Doesn't Matter Anyway*, which is fitting, because to her, it doesn't.

One night my mom and I were sitting out on her big front porch with my brother when she suddenly stated flatly, "We saw that new movie last night."

"What new movie?" asked my brother and I simultaneously.

"Oh, you know," she said airily. "That one with that guy ... *Degrees of Communications!* That's the name of it."

My brother and I exchanged wary glances. Here we go, we thought.

"Are you *sure* that's the name of it?" my brother asked.

"Yep, that's it."

"Who's in it?" I asked, thinking I could do a little detective work without her suspecting.

"Oh, you know, that comedian."

"Which comedian?"

She started to get irritated. "That *comedian*. You *know* his name. Eddie Murphy."

My brother looked at me and his eyebrows disappeared into his hairline. Then he grinned.

"Mom," he started innocently, "was he white?"

"Of *course* he was white!" She was really irritated now. She doesn't like being interrogated by her children, apparently.

"Well, then," my brother began, suppressing a smile, "it wasn't Eddie Murphy."

"Then *who was it?*" She was shouting now.

I was focusing all my energy on not laughing out loud.

"Was there anyone else in the movie?"

"Yes, that girl, that girl that parades around Tokyo in her underwear the whole time!"

Slowly light was beginning to dawn on me.

"Mom," I ventured cautiously, "was this comedian in *Groundhog Day* and *Tootsie?*"

"Yes." Long pause. "I think he was."

"Was it Bill Murray?"

"That's it! I *knew* you'd seen him in a million things."

"Yes, well, but Mom, he isn't *in* any movie called *Degrees of Communications.*"

She glared at me with an I-can-still-turn-you-over-my-knee look. "He absolutely is because I absolutely saw it last night."

My brother and I looked at each other again, and I nodded to him with a you-tell-her-you're-her-favorite look.

"Mom," he gasped through waves of laughter, "you saw *Lost in Translation.* That's what it's called. Not *Degrees of Communications.*"

She paused, her hand on the doorknob. "Oh. Yeah. Okay. That sounds right. I didn't really like it anyway." And she went into the house without a backward glance while my brother and I collapsed into gales of laughter.

My mother is a brilliant and clever thinker and writer, as well as a truly lovely person — and maybe she's right about this: she insists that she can get the words wrong even as she gets the concept right, and that's what matters. She also says that the older she gets, she believes fewer things but with greater intensity. I've heard this called majoring on the majors. Like Ann's "God is" and "God cares," maybe Mom's movie mix-ups are an extension of her evolving theology.

●●●

Whenever my grandmother heard people claim that because they believed in God, they didn't need to worry about getting to know Him, she shot back, "Even the Devil believes in God." Believing *in* God is not that hard. The vast majority of Americans believe in God, or a higher power of some kind. If Sam Harris is to be trusted, it takes more courage and a good deal more integrity *not* to believe.

But what about the times when I, who have been a believer all my life, begin to think that maybe I've made it all up and am just following the crowd, as some would have it? It's funny to me that nonbelievers feel like they are in the minority and believers are the crowd, the "masses" that Karl Marx referred to in his famous statement that religion "is the opium of the people." But most believers feel that they are in the minority, and if the culture put forth by the media is to be believed, it certainly seems like we are.

Sometimes, that other crowd looks awfully appealing, even downright sensible. After all, there are some compelling arguments against God's existence, or at least against a God who is involved, who cares. There are times when I hear more of God's silence than His voice, and that is a hard thing to take when I am in pain, or afraid, or confused. What if those people are right, and I cling to what I believe from fear, or worse, laziness?

Then I hear a voice whisper, "What crowd? Narrow is the road and few are those who find it." I think of my mom's idea that this narrow road is not some grassy path off to the side of the main road but a narrow strip right down the middle of the wide thoroughfare that's going in the opposite direction. So as we walk along it, we have to look into the eyes of those "others" we pass. We have to see them, to touch them as the crowd jostles each other, and so we can't ignore them, can't treat them as though they are on a different trek than us but have to acknowledge that they are fellow sojourners, perhaps going the wrong direction, but worthy of our attention, our voice, our touch, our notice. When I think of it that way, love takes over the fear, and I, like Madeleine, return to the more open spaces of my childlike belief, raising my arms and crying, "I believe; help Thou my unbelief!"

John tells us that when love takes over, there's no

room for fear. Love drives it out. If I fear unbelief—
and worse, unbelievers—then I need love, not debate.
We all need love, believer and unbeliever alike. I pray
for those in search of truth—all of us—that our
search will lead to love.

The fact is, there are days when I don't know what
I believe or why, but my heart does know. Or some
part of me holds onto what I know when my mind lets
loose. And as far as knowing goes, it's called believing
because, in fact, we don't, we can't, *know*; we "hope
in things that are unseen." Maybe knowing with our
minds and knowing with our hearts are often two different things. As Blaise Pascal says, "The heart has its
reasons of which reason knows nothing: we know this
in countless ways." And I think that's okay. After all,
everyone has faith in something, whether it's humanity, fate, the capacity for good, or even in the nonexis-
tence of God. They don't know, in a concrete way, any
more than I do. What I do know is that a life of faith
has so much more hope, so much more joy, so many
more comforts, and sometimes more heartache, than a
life without it. And I choose that, because the moments
when the doubts take over have been the darkest of my
life. Those are the times I know that hell is not so much
a place as it is the absence of God.

●●●

Ann called me yesterday and she blew me away
with this thought: "Being full is not the same thing as
being complete." She said that we can celebrate being

full—of God, of love, of joy, of sorrow, of life—without being complete, which we won't be until Christ returns. But what joy and life we miss when we grieve not being complete instead of celebrating being full. Not being complete, she said, is one of God's great gifts. If we were complete, there would be no room for growing, for learning, or for the joy of becoming full.

Even the incompleteness of not knowing, of periods of unbelief, is a part of this gift from God. If we knew everything, if there were never any doubt, then we wouldn't need to rely on God to lead us when we are unsure, comfort us when we are afraid, or support us when we are falling. Even faith comes from God. Maybe that's why some people don't have it—maybe they don't ask for it.

●●●

My son has a sign on his wall above his desk. It says, "Think. Only fools never doubt." I'm glad he's beginning to learn this now, because I don't want him to panic when doubts come—which they will. Frederick Buechner says, "Whether your faith is that there is a God or that there is not a God, if you don't have any doubts, you are either kidding yourself or asleep. Doubts are the ants in the pants of faith. They keep it awake and moving" (*Wishful Thinking: A Theological ABC*).

When I can't find God, I pray that God will find me. I believe; help my unbelief.

ANGEL

This night I wrestle my angel,
demanding its name
throughout the long hours.
It stares at me with wild eyes,
refusing to be what it is,
refusing to answer the cowardice
of my question. Let me go,
it says, the night is over.
See there; it is light.
I watch the dawn rise,
my questions fade, and I walk on
with neither a limp nor a blessing.

BEING WATER

Around you, a rock at the crest of the fall,
I tumble, changing my shape
to fit the space
When your wood remains too hard to penetrate,
I soak you patiently
until you yield to my press
I melt, ice-like, with the focus of your warmth,
or hover, glasslike, above what's under,
my surface unreadable
I can flow simply through your fingers,
Or erode my surroundings with the force of my
    confinement

I'll make my own way

I evaporate in a drought

These are the privileges of being water

I bubble or crash
I boil or freeze
I cool or drown
I flow around or into

I flow
I receive
I pour myself out,
quenching your thirst

13

WISDOM

For as long as I can remember, I've desired wisdom. That I'm not even sure what that means is part of the fascination: trying to understand what it means to be wise, chasing down the image so I can sketch it for future reference. Sometimes I think I have it, and then it disappears around a corner.

Last year we toured a manor home called Athelhampton in Dorset, England. It's known primarily for its stunning gardens and its ghost: a former pet ape who, the story goes, died of a broken heart after its master's death and now makes regular appearances to startled visitors. We admired the house and grounds, and though we didn't see the ape, a heavy oak and iron door opened apparently by itself, scaring the pants off our youngest son.

One of the many gardens is a formal, Italianate sunken garden, flanked on all four sides by enormous obelisk-shaped arbor vitae. Our kids played hide-and-seek among these giant shrubs while I snapped pictures. In one, a pedestaled fountain in the lawn is the centerpiece, while the figure of my little boy darts out of the corner of the frame like a garden gnome.

The boy is wisdom; the fountain is where I'm usually looking for it.

●●●

In *Conversations*, Eugene Peterson shares his thoughts about how he paraphrased the book of Proverbs, a book that speaks a great deal about wisdom. " 'Wisdom' is the biblical term for this on-earth-as-it-is-in-heaven everyday living. Wisdom is the art of living skillfully in whatever actual conditions we find ourselves."

I don't know about you, but I often find myself in situations in which I am unsure, stuck, or otherwise unclear about how to behave wisely. These past few months have been the most difficult in my life as a parent. There were times when I turned in desperation to those people who embody wisdom for me. Sometimes that person is Ann, who always seems to strike the right balance between humor, delight, empathy, logic, peace, and compassion. She seems to know just when to call, like the day she called when I was at my lowest, "just to hear my voice." I poured out my heartache as a mom to her, and she listened carefully, as she always does, before responding with a simple assignment: "Write down everything good that has happened in this terrible season. Then, during these times when you can't see God's hand, read back through them and you will have proof that He is at work."

Sometimes that embodiment of wisdom is a saint like Julian of Norwich, whom I've read about. She wouldn't "treat" anyone spiritually until they had been fed and rested, because she believed no one can heal spiritually until they are ministered to in basic physical ways. She was centuries ahead of her time in the field of psychological health. She reminds me, like the ravens who visited Elijah, that I can't do the work I have been given to do without food for my body, a good night's sleep, and the life-giving realization of God's indescribable love for me. In the worst of times, I hear her voice echoing down through the centuries like waves on the shore: "All shall be well and all shall be well and all manner of things shall be well."

Sometimes it's someone like Henri Nouwen or Brennan Manning, known to me only through their writings or speaking, working patiently and graciously with the downtrodden, the outcast, the sick. The days that I feel underappreciated, overworked, or even abused, I think of their stamina, their compassion, and their belief in the human capacity for dignity and for God. I think of Henri living day after day with the severely handicapped at the Daybreak Community, or Brennan ministering to the addicts, constantly reminding him of himself, and I find strength to carry on with the laundry or the cooking or the writing or the hard work of training up a child.

Sometimes it's my friend and spiritual director Sister Mildred at the Benedictine community an hour away. I go see her when I'm in a muddle and need help sorting through things. She has that same gentle balance that Ann has, with a dash of old-fashioned Indiana farm-girl sensibility. (She reminds me of my "country" grandma, my dad's mom, only with two or three PhDs.) I sat with her in a garden swing on the monastery grounds one beautiful day last summer and told her the long story of a friend whom I love and didn't know how to help. She listened and asked hard questions about my role in this friend's life, gently prodding my weary heart toward the realization that I cannot, nor should I, take on another's burden. It is one thing to help each other with a heavy load, she said, but quite another to take from someone what they must learn to carry on their own or else put down. They can learn it no other way.

● ● ●

When I look at what all these people seem to have in common, I see some patterns: ready tears and laughter; the ability to see things from another's point of view; the ability to feel another's pain; enjoyment of the humor or absurdity in a situation, and the grace to point it out with gentleness; the skill of knowing one's own limits; generosity of spirit and gifts; comfort in his or her own skin; a lack of jealousy; a disciplined life. In short, they have developed a sense of balance, which might be the best definition of wisdom. All things in balance is the opposite of the bloated excess that is foolishness.

Wisdom understands that life is both tragedy and

comedy, humor and pathos, like a good play or movie. Every moment contains the capacity for joy or for heartbreak, and this very tension is what makes life so full. Life positively vibrates with possibility. The human condition is fraught with meaning, and if it was worthy of God's full attention, isn't it worthy of ours?

Children, as well as new believers, seem to have a better sense of this balance than most adults. In our experience in house church, it is often one of the children, or one of the new Christians, who says the wise thing, which — let's face it — is very often the obvious thing. A wise friend of mine challenges me to state the truth in the simplest terms when I am facing something overwhelming. "I feel afraid." "Your words hurt me." "If the worst thing happens, I will still be okay." Children know instinctively that sometimes the wisest thing to say or do is staring us in the face.

One night at house church, a man was pouring out his heart about a personal and difficult issue. We listened with sympathy and concern, feeling helpless and unsure of what to say or do. Finally one of the younger children, who clearly had no idea of what was happening in grown-up terms, said simply, "Why don't we just pray for him?" So we did. Our spirit of helplessness was lifted.

My youngest son is often wise beyond his years. I was putting him to bed the other night, trying to get him to quit bouncing around long enough so I could ask him if he had already brushed his teeth. Finally, I got his attention, and he suddenly stopped bouncing and answered breathlessly, "Yes, I brushed my teeth, but I want to know: is *love* a noun or a verb?"

"Ah," I said, trying to sound wise. "You have asked the question of the century, my son. *I* think," drawing it out for emphasis, "that it is both."

A moment of silence while he pondered this.

"I *knew* it," he said, looking smug. "I knew it was both, because it is something you can *have*, but it is also something you can *do*."

Once, when my daughter was about four years old, we were in the bathtub together. I was washing her hair, and we were singing a children's song that includes the line, "Jesus, You sure must love me a lot."

"Do you know that, Madeleine? Do you know He loves you a lot?" I said, as I poured warm water over her hair, tipping her head back to keep the soap out of her eyes.

Without opening her eyes, her head resting in my hands trustingly, she said, "*Mommy.* Of *course* I know that. He is the *Good Shepherd*. We're His *sheep*. He knows us by *name*."

How could I be so foolish to question it?

● ● ●

Other times it is the question of a new believer that brings life and truth into our midst, blowing away the cobwebs of stunted thinking and tired jargon. I love it when someone who didn't grow up in the church comes into our lives and our gatherings; their insights and questions don't fit into anyone's collection of accepted words and phrases. They just say it or ask it, and it feels like someone has opened a window and a fresh breeze of truth blows in. Our dear friend Heather first came to know Jesus the summer after we graduated from college. I had been married just over a year, and she came to live with us for a few months. Her hunger for God and for Scripture was contagious and exciting. She often blew us away with her insights as she dug deeper and deeper into the truth of God. One evening she called to me from her room. When I walked in, she was looking in amazement at me, her Bible open on her lap. "I just figured out why Jesus had to come. Because being good isn't good enough." I stared back at her, dumbfounded, new revelations breaking over me as well.

Fast-forward ten years: Heather's daughter Varland has had, for as long as she's been able to talk, a desire for the things of God. One Sunday morning, when she was about two, Heather took her to the altar for communion. As the minister handed out the elements, saying, "This is the body of Christ, broken for you; this is the blood of Christ, shed for you," she solemnly held out her hands for the wafer and dipped it carefully in the cup, and then bowed her head. But when Heather picked her up to take her back to her seat, she began to cry and strain against her mother, reaching desperately for the altar. "More Christ!" she wailed. "More Christ!"

What if we all responded to Christ's offerings with that kind of hunger for more? Would our capacity for wisdom grow, like Grandma's vat of glory? One thing is for sure: we wouldn't remain the same.

● ● ●

Wisdom is fluid. It has to be, because life is too.

Consider "flip-flopping" in politics. Shouldn't we be more fearful of a leader who refuses to learn, to grow, to change, and to receive new information? Having convictions can be a strength, but refusing to learn is laziness, and worse, a lack of compassion and humility.

Humility is a key to unlock wisdom. Am I wise enough to know I don't know? Humble enough to ask for wisdom? "The fear of God," Scripture says, "is the beginning of wisdom." The beginning, not the end. And woe to me if I think I have a handle on this thing called life. Let me begin with the admission that I can't do it on my own, and maybe, just maybe, I will begin to develop some wisdom.

● ● ●

My grandpa George was a picture of wisdom. He is my model for discipline, which is part of what made him wise. He farmed and worked nights at an automobile battery factory until his retirement, after which he continued to farm and began touring with my parents, managing the record tables at their concerts. He did this for thirty years. At age ninety, he developed cancer and left the road for good. He died peacefully a year later, his garden, yard, and home carefully maintained.

He was a quiet man with a dry wit. He had an open and sincere curiosity about anything he didn't know: a new engine; an ethnic cuisine he had never tried; an unfamiliar culture or race; a newfangled gadget. He didn't say much and never felt the need to comment like I do; he would tell you what he thought only if you begged him, and sometimes not even then.

My dad tells the story of living in the little rental house next door when he and my mom were first married. My dad had purchased his first lawn mower and left it out before leaving for the evening. On their way in the car with my grandfather that night, it started to rain. My father asked Grandpa, "Dad, will the rain hurt my new mower?"

Grandpa chewed thoughtfully on his toothpick.

"It won't help it," he said.

"I know that, Dad. But will it hurt it?"

"It won't help it," he repeated patiently.

My dad began to get frustrated.

"I *know* it won't help, Dad. That's not what I'm asking. Will it *hurt* it?"

"Well," began my grandpa, "it won't—"

"Dad," my father interrupted in exasperation, "would *you* have left *your* mower out if it was going to rain?"

Grandpa looked straight out the front window and replied levelly, "Not on your life."

I remember Grandpa walking his garden in the spring, planning his rows, chewing on his toothpick. His garden was legendary, and when my grandmother was alive, the garden meals that came from it were legendary too. She'd call us on a summer day, mid-morning, to tell us that she had a "big pot of beans on," which meant she had cooked green beans stocked with new potatoes and carrots, all picked by her and Grandpa that morning. At lunch there would be a stack of plates and forks, a pitcher of fresh limeade, a platter of sliced garden tomatoes, and a big cut-glass bowl of cottage cheese, all set out on the counter for whoever wanted it. Sometimes, if we didn't finish it all off at lunch, we'd come back at dinnertime and eat the same thing.

Grandpa's knowledge about gardening and the cycles of the earth was undisputed; after all, didn't he have the biggest and most productive garden, the best beef cows, and the prettiest yard, shaded by mellowed and flaking silver and red maples? He understood his own rhythms too. Home or on the road, he rose early, stopped after two cups of coffee, worked hard all morning, rested after lunch, drank water when he was thirsty, never overate, worked all afternoon, and went to bed at the same time every night, even if it was in a bunk on the bus.

He was also very practical. He did the obvious thing. Before I was born, Grandpa was a smoker. He used to smoke unfiltered Camels when he worked out in the field. Grandma wouldn't have cigarettes in the house, and I don't think he thought much of them either, if he was indoors. Sometime in the sixties, when the surgeon general began putting on cigarette boxes the warning that smoking could cause cancer, Grandma noticed that she hadn't seen Grandpa's cigarettes around lately. When she asked him about it, he said without any explanation that he had quit. She asked him when, and he said, "About three weeks ago." Apparently he had noticed the warnings and without any discussion or equivocation decided to quit. That was how he did things. He didn't take unnecessary risks, and he didn't waste energy with indecision. He kept a toothpick in his mouth from then on; I don't remember him ever being without one. He twirled it between his fingers and munched thoughtfully on it when he was pondering something.

He planted his garden by the moon and *The Farmer's Almanac*. He raised cows, used the manure for fertilizer, mulched with bags of cut grass, and fed the spent vegetable plants back to the cows. For him, it was a simple and self-evident cycle.

When I was planting my first garden, I followed him around his garden with a notebook, asking his advice for what and when to plant. He was never one to give advice, solicited or otherwise, and it was like trying to get blood out of a turnip. I don't think he was trying to thwart me; the things of the earth were second nature to him, and putting them into step-by-step instructions was like trying to explain breathing to someone with gills.

I asked him about where I should plant peas in relation to corn: would it matter? Are there certain plants you shouldn't put next to onions? How do you keep rabbits and deer out of the garden? (He planted a row of marigolds around the edges.) When do you put out beans? Tomatoes? Lettuce? Potatoes?

"Good Friday," he answered to this last question.

"You have to do it on Good Friday?" I asked hurrying along behind him, trying to write this morsel of wisdom into my notebook.

"That's just when I've always done it. 'Course, you don't wanna plant potatoes by the dark of the moon. You gotta check the *Almanac.*"

"Why? You can't plant potatoes by the dark of the moon?" Did I even believe this? Grandpa wasn't one for superstition.

"You can. You can do anything you want." He paused, chewing on his toothpick. "But they won't come up anything but tops."

"Have you done it, Grandpa?"

"Yep. Once."

"And what happened? What does 'just tops' mean?"

He turned back to the shed, as though he had said all there was to say on the matter.

"No potatoes," he said over his shoulder.

I remember another time I went out to his garden to try to glean some wisdom. He was there, pacing the rows, checking the progress. I noticed very few weeds. Having just experienced my first summer of the uphill battle to keep weeds out of my flowerbeds, I thought he must have some shortcut method, perhaps some chemical he sprayed (of which I did not approve).

Casually I asked, "How do you keep the weeds out, Grandpa?"

He stopped and looked at me with puzzlement and surprise.

"Hoe 'em out. How do you think?"

When my dad was a young man, traveling evangelists came through town to preach at his church. Once, during the Korean War, an itinerant preacher talked about the end of the world and why he believed the time was ripe for the second coming. It worried my dad.

He came home and found my grandpa in the garden, hoeing out the weeds between the rows.

"Dad," my father began, "that preacher ... he said this might be the end of the world."

"Yeah," Grandpa said, stopping his work to wipe his brow with his handkerchief. "They've been sayin' that for a long time. And one of these days they're gonna be right." He grinned his signature grin. "But in the meantime, I gotta get these weeds outta this garden."

And he went back to his steady work.

There is a simple wisdom in this philosophy of life. I call it In the Meantime. One day we will be redeemed; one day Jesus will come; one day everything will be explained. In the meantime, however, there's work to be done. Aren't there people to be loved? Isn't there pain to be alleviated, suffering to be comforted, wisdom to be sought, justice to work toward, and joy to be found?

When Grandpa died, people came from all over the country to pay their respects. He had a wide circle of friends and admirers, from the UPS man to musicians to childhood friends. Many people spoke at his funeral, telling funny stories or sharing their appreciation of his wry wit, his patience, his gentle humor, and his steadfastness. I was privileged to write the following and share it with his friends and family.

WAIT AND SEE

For Grandpa George

For those who knew my grandfather well, one of the things that stood out about him most was his "wait and see" attitude. He lived a life of integrity and honor, not a little bit due to his ability—no, choice—to wait and see what the outcome would be on any number of things.

If questioned about his choice for candidate in political office—no doubt a conservative choice made with conservative emotion—he would squint at the TV and say cautiously, "Well, we'll see, won't we?"

When I asked him if he thought I'd made a good choice on the horse I'd saved for and bought as a preteen, he fiddled with his toothpick while he walked around my horse sizing him up, saying only, "We'll just have to wait and see."

He seemed to look at grandchildren and

great-grandchildren with a combination of pride, interest, amusement, and just a touch of "we'll wait and see."

Most of his decisions — financial, emotional, political, even romantic and spiritual — seemed to be made with this philosophical and practical approach to life. I can just imagine my grandmother saying to him for the first time with heartfelt ardor, "I'll love you forever, George," and him squinting back at her, fiddling with his toothpick, and replying, "Well, we'll see."

There remains a small mystery about what went on in the heart of this farmer and tool-and-die maker with his German roots, his interested and sharp mind, and his dry wit. Those of us who knew him best never heard him talk about heaven, God, or matters of the soul, though he surrounded himself with those who talked and sang about it almost constantly. He lived a faithful life. He loved and cared for his wife for sixty-seven years; he buried two children and raised three, then helped raise two grandchildren; he walked the rows of his religiously tended garden, raised four cows every year, planted potatoes by the phase of the moon, and lived by the *Almanac* — all the while traveling on the weekends with his singing son and managing the record tables for thirty-three years. This is a life worthy of our honor.

And while it might surprise you to hear that I myself have more of this "wait and see" attitude than I'd like to admit, I don't think it will surprise anyone that I believe Grandpa's wait is over, that I've watched him all my life, thinking, "Wait and see, Grandpa. Wait and see." That he has waited, with patience and grace, and that he now, at last, sees.

Each of us must wait and see what happens next when we've been planting and sowing. Part of wisdom, I learned from Grandpa and from others, is learning how to wait with patience, and the willingness to change while we wait.

After the funeral, my sister and I were talking to Ann. How, my sister asked, can we know what went on in Grandpa's heart? How do we know he knew Jesus? He never said anything directly about it that we knew of.

Ann thought quietly for a moment, and for a split second I saw the image of my grandpa chewing thoughtfully on his toothpick.

"Well," she said, a smile crinkling her blue eyes, "Jesus said we will know the tree by its fruits."

My sister and I looked at each other, unsure where she was going with this. A garden metaphor? Something to do with Grandpa's yard?

Ann searched out our eyes, giving us time to catch on. Then she began this list: "Love, joy, peace, patience, gentleness, self-control, goodness, kindness, faithfulness."

She smiled as the tears sprang to our eyes in recognition of our grandfather. "Do any of these sound familiar?"

• • •

What I'm really after is the kind of wisdom that bears fruit, that grows the good stuff. I want a rich harvest — not money and houses and more stuff, but kids who know who and whose they are; a long and rich marriage; a resume of faithfulness; a reputation for joy and delight and humor and gentleness and hard work; a full orchard of abundant life, here on earth as it is in heaven. I long to see my roots grow deeper and deeper into the rich loam of God's grace.

This, I think, is wisdom: to cultivate a full harvest of love, joy, peace, patience, gentleness, self-control, goodness, kindness, faithfulness.

Isn't this what each of us longs for? Do any of these sound familiar?

MY GRANDFATHER'S GARDEN

Here was my grandfather's garden:
four rows of tasseled corn, three
of tomatoes, two of sweet climbing
peas, and four of beans, now waxing
yellow in the late autumn sun.
Zinnias, lined in parade formation,
cornflowers looped like a lavender
moat around the vegetables.
My grandmother spent her summers here:
picked, canned, froze, fresh-cooked
pot after simmering pot brimming
with beans, the pungent steam
fogging the close cellar air.
Now this garden marks the seasons,
shrinking every year; rows shorten and plants
are pulled to feed the cows. Rhubarb,
once the southern border, runs riot
in a sea of grass and weeds, unpicked
and uncanned.
My grandfather walks the rows,
stooped, all movement and no philosophy,
shaking down black bags of grass clippings,
shoveling on barrows of manure.
This is a cycle without a goal, a physical
lament, an elegy hoed beneath the leaves
of every tired, wandering plant.

39

This day I celebrate the day I came
yelling and wriggling to this tired earth
the day I took my first gulp of
clean, ripe air.
I came through my mother, from her
but then I had to work things out
as just me and now it is almost forty
years of this working out, this —
oh, who am I kidding —
most of it has been a party
and instead of wondering when the
fun will begin I'm wondering if
things ever get really serious.
Honestly, it's more joy than I
thought there would be and anyway —
if I have to grow up
(forty sounds very serious)
if I have to grow up
better I have one more year to laugh
it all off and enjoy stuff before
entering my Most Grown-Up Year,
pushing down my dress and suppressing a grin.

14

FEAST

I fell in love with Andrew, my husband, initially because he cooked for me. Our first real date was at his apartment, to which he invited me for dinner. I assumed a young man living alone would live in comfortable squalor, a sort of organized mess, and that he would rustle up macaroni and cheese from a box, maybe with ice cream from a carton. I was prepared to be underwhelmed and kindly appreciative. I arrived, a little curious and not a little nervous, at a spotless (read: so clean you could eat off the floor) and tidy apartment in which he had, with apparent ease and considerable élan, made for me Italian seafood (lobster) casserole, Caesar salad, crusty garlic bread, and chocolate mousse, all from scratch. I ate, stunned and humbled, at a simply but beautifully laid table, complete with cloth napkins and lit candles. He was a complete gentleman, as he is now.

I know. I'm lucky. I won't say that his food is the only thing that made me fall in love with him, but I will say that it got my attention. After that, I listened to him read poetry, learned about his favorite authors and composers, and pretty well went anywhere he wanted to take me. That first meal was the beginning of the opening of my heart, and it's been opening ever since. He's still cooking for me, and I for him, and food is one of our favorite languages of love.

I often wonder how our relationship would have been different, if indeed it would have been given birth at all, had I not accepted that first invitation, or if our first date had been in a restaurant somewhere. No doubt it would have been a pleasant meal, and no doubt there would have been other invitations, but the fact that our first meal was private, the labor of his own hands only for me, set a precedent in our relationship and in our subsequent marriage for servanthood, his for me and mine for him, with seldom a thought of entitlement or scorekeeping. In many ways, that first meal demonstrated for me that Andrew's idea of marriage closely mirrored Christ's love for His disciples the night He washed their feet. I remember that first meal together in that quiet and simple apartment whenever I think about that moment before the Last Supper — that moment of complete and utter humility, and the disciples' surprise and wonder at the required response of acceptance. Acceptance of grace is a humbling act, and one that requires far too much humility and far more relinquishment of control than many of us are willing to make. I am amazed I had the wisdom at that point in my life to accept it; I am so grateful I did.

•••

I always know when Andrew is stressed out and struggling to deal with his stress. He takes over the kitchen and begins several cooking projects at once. One day I came home from teaching and found him simmering a huge pot of spaghetti sauce, stirring a large batch of spicy chili, and chopping vegetables for a crock-pot vegetable beef soup. He was chopping with such concentration, his lower jaw jutting out to warn me I had better leave him to it and let him work through his stress. I went upstairs. That evening we had a good supper of chili and cornbread and I noticed his jaw had relaxed and the lines between his eyes had smoothed out.

Cooking is creative therapy for him, and for me too. We work peacefully and happily together in the kitchen, often at the same time, because we work in different realms. He tends to make complicated sauces and complicated dishes that require several processes, like chicken picatta and béarnaise sauce. I tend to bake. The visceral feel of the dough, elastic and responsive, in my floured and sticky hands; the muscle a good bread demands to become compliant; the fragile combination of flour, butter, and sugar in a good scone or biscuit, mixed to just barely hold together; the raw and decadent temptation of a Toll House or Christmas sugar-cookie dough — these are the creations that soothe my worried mind and furrowed brow. I'm not sure what it is about these rituals that is balm to my spirit and my stomach, but there is something about the connection between mind and body, the path from

mind to hand to oven or stove to stomach, that somehow, magically, makes its warming way into the soul.

●●●

Many years ago my parents and some of their
friends started a weekend event in Indianapolis called
Praise Gathering, which quickly became a unique and
beloved national event every fall for thirty-three years.
One year after one of the very last Praise Gatherings,
I wrote this piece to explain my love of this event and
of the restlessness and angst that inevitably ensued at
its close.

THE POST-PRAISE GATHERING BAKE-OFF

I don't know about you, but getting home
from Praise Gathering is always a bit traumatic
for me. Even my kids feel anxiety leaving the
hallowed grounds of downtown Indianapolis. My eight-year-old son whines, "Why do
we have to wait a whole year between Praise
Gatherings?" I feebly answer something about
it not being special otherwise, like Christmas,
but inwardly I feel his pain.

We walk through the convention center
Sunday morning on our way to breakfast and
I watch as the facility staff takes down signs
and pulls up carpet, resetting rooms for some
new expo. Colts fans and their families saunter
happily through, anticipating the afternoon's
game. My husband remarks he'd like to come

sometime for a big car or book show. The words "merchants in the temple" flash through my brain. Doesn't he know? This is sacred ground.

But the reality is, of course, that it's just a building. It's no more sacred than the bricks or cinder blocks that hold us in on Sunday mornings. What makes it sacred to me, and to thousands of others, is what happens there every fall from a Thursday to Saturday night in October, as much a part of the season as harvest and Thanksgiving. What makes it sacred is who visits with us. Maybe He hangs around for the car and book shows. Who knows?

What I do know and have learned to expect is the feeling of—what? emptiness, maybe—when I get home on Sunday afternoon. It feels as if the fires have all gone out in my belly and I'm bone cold and a little panicked. Other than having a nap, I'm never quite sure what to do with myself. I'm never ready to leave Indianapolis, the convention center, my hotel room. But these places, of course, don't stay the same either. The faces change; the rooms get cleaned; the new convention comes in. Obviously, the mystery doesn't happen because of the place. Where do I find it, then, and how do I hold onto it once I'm out of that mystical environment and back in the mundane?

I call my sister Sunday night and have to laugh. We are both baking, lighting candles, cocooning with our families. They had been, after all, with us in Indianapolis too. In absence of each other, she and I are calling people who have also been there, to kibbitz, to process, to remember; we're like tribes around our campfires after the ceremony. I ask her, "How many people do you think are back home tonight after Praise Gathering lighting things and baking?"

"I don't know," she answers. "We should take a poll."

I call more people. Yes, they say, they have the candles or the fire lit. "What are you doing now?" I ask.

"Well ... it's funny. I don't usually bake, but I had this cookie dough ..."

I sit down next to the fire with our children and read them a chapter from *The Secret Garden*. The smell of wood smoke penetrates the membranes of my nose, curls into my brain, warming the cold places and soothing the anxiety of returning to my life. I am thankful the weather has turned cold. A fire will feel good these chilly fall nights. We will need the fire to warm us, to coax us back to our own hearth. We will need our warm food too, straight from the oven or the stove, because it will bring the warmth into us, like communion, feeding the cinders still glowing inside us. That's it, I suddenly think; we don't want the fire to go out.

I take a warm chocolate chip cookie, contemplating the vegetable soup I'll start in the
morning. We'll eat together again tomorrow
night, relighting the fires in our souls, knowing
each other again, nesting warmly in our love
for each other, lighting our candles of remembrance so we won't forget. Maybe next year
we'll build the fire before we leave on Thursday, so it will be waiting for the lit match when
we return. Next year, I think, maybe I'll bake
an apple pie.

● ● ●

There is a beautiful Danish movie called *Babette's
Feast*. In it, a gifted cook named Babette spends her
entire and unexpected inheritance on a feast she
decides to prepare for all her friends. Like other "foodie
movies," such as *Big Night* and *Like Water for Chocolate*, there is an element of magic in the food's ability
to dissolve old grudges, ignite long-dead romance, and
kindle new love. It is a movie partly about the connection between the food that we put into our bodies and
the food for the soul that it becomes when it is prepared
in love and shared with friends. But this movie's feast
is a particularly lovely and poignant picture of grace.
As I once heard it put, "Wherever grace is spent, it is
squandered." In other words, grace is grace *because* it
is a feast we didn't prepare, we didn't pay for, we aren't
worthy of eating, and we don't have to clean up. If any
part of it were deserved, it wouldn't be grace. It's all a
feast. And we've been invited.

My mother loves to read this piece from Bob Benson's *Laughter in the Walls,* and I love it too. He says it better here than anything else I've ever seen on the subject. And he uses — what else? — food to do it.

SUNDAY SCHOOL PICNIC

Do you remember when they had old-fashioned Sunday school picnics? It was before air-conditioning. They said, "We'll meet at Sycamore Lodge in Shelby Park at 4:30 Saturday. You bring your supper and we'll furnish the tea."

But you came home at the last minute and when you got ready to pack your lunch, all you could find in the refrigerator was one dried-up piece of baloney and just enough mustard in the bottom of the jar so that you got it all over your knuckles trying to get to it. And there were just two stale pieces of bread. So, you made your baloney sandwich and wrapped it in some brown bag and went to the picnic.

When it came time to eat, you sat at the end of a table and spread out your sandwich. But the folks next to you — the lady was a good cook and she had worked all day and she had fried chicken, baked beans and potato salad and homemade rolls and sliced tomatoes and pickles and olives and celery and topped it off with two big homemade chocolate pies. And they spread it all out beside you. And there you were with your baloney sandwich.

But they said to you, "Why don't we put it all together?" "No, I couldn't do that, I just couldn't even think of it," you murmured, embarrassed.

"Oh, come on! There's plenty of chicken and plenty of pie, and plenty of everything — and we just love baloney sandwiches. Let's just put it all together." And so you did and there you sat — eating like a king when you came like a pauper.

And I get to thinking. I think of me "sharing in the very being of God" (2 Peter 1:4 NEB). When I think of how little I bring, and how much He brings and that He invites me to "share," I know I should be shouting from the housetops but I am so filled with awe and wonder that I can hardly be heard.

I know you don't have enough love and faith, or grace, or mercy or wisdom. But He has. He has all those things in abundance and says, "Let's just put it all together. Everything I possess is available to you. Everything I am and can be to a person, I will be to you."

When I think about it like that, it really amuses me to see somebody running along through life hanging onto their dumb bag with that stale baloney sandwich, saying, "God's not going to get my sandwich! No siree, this is mine!" Did you ever see anybody like that? So needy — just about half-starved to death, hanging on for dear life? It's not that He needs your sandwich. The fact is, you need His chicken.

—Bob Benson

I love that picture of grace—the table spread, the invitation issued. Why wouldn't I accept?

●●●

I have a number of favorite foods and food experiences. I dearly love white wedding cake, and will travel miles and miles to a wedding in anticipation of this promised favorite. I adore my husband's chicken picatta, lemony and crisp on the outside, juicy and tender in the middle, and his creamy and surprisingly spicy béarnaise sauce, which has ruined me for anyone else's. I really appreciate a good, basic Bolognese sauce done really well. It's always the first thing I order when I visit a new Italian restaurant; I figure if they get that right, everything else they do will be good as well.

Give me a saltshaker, and you can't beat a ripe Indiana tomato, straight from the garden and warm from the sun. There is something about the alkaline Indiana clay, hard as it is to deal with, that makes the world's most perfect tomatoes. I remember the sweet and tart taste of my grandmother's black raspberry pie, right out of the oven, so hot it burnt my tongue, and the first time I had afternoon tea in England when I was ten: the new taste of hot tea served in a real teacup and saucer, cooled with milk and sweetened with sugar and taken with a chocolate-covered cookie they called a biscuit, sent me into spasms of delight.

I've always felt like I lived in the wrong country for breakfast; I've never loved typical American breakfast foods. I loved it when my parents took me to Europe when I was a child and I discovered that many Europeans breakfast on warm bread, mild cheese, homemade yogurt, and fresh fruit. Many years later, the morning after arriving in Japan late the evening before, I awoke dreading the breakfast experience, expecting raw fish or egg. I was delighted to discover instead a beautiful tray of little compartments, each one containing something fragrant and delicious: a strip of scrambled egg; a round bowl of perfectly steamed white rice; a tiny fillet of hot grilled white fish; a little salad of mixed lettuce and cucumber; a small bowl of miso soup; and a handle-less cup of green tea. I was in heaven, and ever since, my husband painstakingly recreates that breakfast and brings it to my bed on a tray every Mother's Day and birthday. Bless him.

The summer he and I were first married, we vacationed with my family in Nantucket. Because most of the island was filled with my family's memories, my family wanted to give us a memory that would be only ours. They sent us for dinner at a beautiful restaurant called the Summer House in Sconset, an elegant area of the island. I'm not sure if that meal is so memorable because I was a newlywed, or because it was my first grown-up romantic memory with my husband in this domain of childhood memories, or because the food was so good. I do know the food was truly exceptional, and the atmosphere, the view of the ocean, and the grand piano played by an excellent musician in the corner all made for one of those meals that will live on in the annuls of our marriage. It was also the first time I tried crème brulee, which has become, needless to say for anyone who has ever tried it, the Cadillac of all desserts for me, second only to, say, a really moist and light white wedding cake with butter cream icing and almond flavoring.

Almost every meal we had in Italy had the same effect on me; I actually teared up over a plate of pasta with a walnut sauce I can't even begin to describe, in spite of a long search to recreate it. One night in Italy, our friend David ordered a pork loin, which was actually wild boar that had been shot locally that morning in a nearby wood. If you've never had wild boar in Italy, I urge you to book your plane ticket now. We all sampled it, and after mostly moans of pleasure and eye-rolling ecstasy, Andrew made up a sort of aria about pork, in which the main word was, as I remember it, *pork*, and which we all sang to the waiter, who bore it more or less graciously, nodding sagely as though he got this sort of thing all the time.

Last January we took a group of students to Athens for a study of ancient Greek theater. On our final night, we were taken by our hosts to a traditional taverna where we were all given a choice of four roasted meats: chicken, beef, lamb, or rabbit. We all agreed to have a bit of each from each other's plates, and I can honestly say it was the best meat I've ever had in my life, all of it. Each was different, but flavorful, tender, perfect. After dinner, the servers brought platters of sliced apples and oranges, sprinkled with walnuts and drizzled with honey. So simple. Heaven.

I often think about my love of good food. I love to flip through good cookbooks to be inspired, and to plan meals for my family or friends. I love the creativity of cooking for Andrew, and the quiet companionship of cooking with him. I love preparing food that I or someone I know grew, fed, watered, nurtured, or butchered. I love the idea that food I labored over is nourishing my family. I love that God provides it for me in the hope that I will be delighted, fed, and grateful, and that I will not abuse it. I think He wants me to take delight in the variety, the simplicity, the genius of the food He has spread for me, and to see it as a metaphor for the family feast that He has laid for each of us, and that place at the table that only you, or I, can fill.

● ● ●

Let me tell you about how we celebrate Thanksgiving in my family. It has become my favorite holiday, not because I don't love celebrating my Savior's birth (I love it!) or His resurrection but because Thanksgiving is, for us, about so much more than the food. It has become a time to contemplate and articulate, to realize and to give voice to, the ways in which God has visibly and miraculously worked in the past year. But let me back up; for us, the ritual of Thanksgiving starts earlier in the week, usually on the Tuesday before Thanksgiving Thursday.

Our university breaks for the holiday on the Tuesday before, and so, thankfully, do our children's schools. We usually pick them up after school and head straight up to my parents' house, about a two-hour drive from our house. On the way, we stop at a big Whole Foods store in Indianapolis and pick up a huge, twenty-five-pound organic free-range turkey, which is our contribution to the feast. We arrive at my parents' house after dark, where all the candles are lit, fragrant soup is simmering on the stove, and the table is laid for us. We are usually the first of the "kids" to arrive for the festivities, so we have my parents and their house to ourselves for a night.

The next morning, my mother and I begin work on the baking, while the men and big boys start moving furniture around to accommodate the extra tables and people that will arrive later. They clear off the huge central counter in my mother's kitchen, and start checking off tasks on the "honey do" list my mother makes for them, carrying boxes of papers, cards, mail, canisters, and other items that normally litter my mother's kitchen down to the basement and temporarily out of sight.

My mother and I spend the afternoon setting tables all over the house: the long, formal dining room table with the black octagonal dishes and the pheasant placemats; the big oak kitchen table with the traditional cream and brown dishes and brown glass goblets; the long folding table in my parents' large bedroom with the white Nantucket basket-weave china; a round folding table in the living room for the teenagers, with the everyday dishes; and two small children's tables in the family room with child-size plates and placemats for the little ones. We laugh and talk, organize and shout questions and answers back and forth to each other as we work. The kids (and husbands) all disappear to hang out with my sister or brother somewhere else so we can work without fear of dirt or breakage. It's one of my favorite days of the year, making beauty, smelling tomorrow's delicacies, and having my mother to myself, which is a rarity since I've had children.

About bedtime we hover over the sink and prepare the enormous turkey for the oven, stuffing it with chopped apples and onions, butter, salt, and pepper. We fasten a huge poultry bag around it, shove it into the wall oven, and go to bed, leaving it to slow cook in a medium oven. I know, as I am awakened throughout the night by the bird's aroma, that my mother will be up before dawn to turn the oven down to warm, baste the turkey, and allow it to "rest" in its own juice until my husband carves it, dripping and tender, at about eleven.

People start arriving about then, and that's when it gets interesting. As each family arrives, bearing food, coats, and children, they wander the house, tapping into the hot apple cider percolating on the sideboard and snacking on olives and carrot sticks. Once we've all gathered around the large farm kitchen (usually about thirty of us), one of the children passes around a little turkey-shaped basket full of kernels of Indian corn. Each person takes one, which represents the less-than-ample first Thanksgiving feast, at which each person was allotted five kernels of corn for the day, and there was much grieving for the dead and many prayers said for the ill and dying. I love that we take this time and perform this gesture not only to remember the origin of this most American of holidays but to remind ourselves of its roots in the birth of our nation itself.

In this soil of remembrance and sobriety, we plant the seeds of a year's worth of blessings, victories, and gratitude. As we pass the basket around the circle, each person drops their kernel in and says aloud to the circle full of people we've grown up with, people who've raised us and been witness to our choices and their outcomes, friends without a family circle who, for various reasons, would otherwise be alone on this family holiday, the things for which he or she is most grateful this season. Each year the circle grows, enlarged by those who have gone on, leaving their presence and our memories of them behind, and by those who are invited, and by those who have come lately, "trailing clouds of glory," as Wordsworth says, from heaven, born into this circle of people who will love them, raise them, and bear witness to their choices and their outcomes. We speak and give testimony to the workings of God in our lives over the past year, the people for whom we are thankful, the events that marked and defined our year, and the hopes and dreams for the future, for our children and parents, and for our country.

This ritual, part harvest and part sowing, gives rise to the prayer that my father prays before we all, cleansed, cried, and hungry, collect a plate from a place laid just for us, and file into the long line past the makeshift buffet on the big square kitchen counter. We pile on Grandma's green beans, creamy mashed potatoes, and homemade chicken and noodles, now made by my cousin Becky; my mother's oyster dressing, cheesy Brussels sprouts, turkey, salads, and warm rolls; my sister's baked yellow squash and zucchini; my uncle Dave's artfully created crudités plate; and Aunt MaryAnn's broccoli-and-rice casserole (hurry, it'll be gone). For dessert, there are my brother-in-law's mother's famous chocolate pies, my mother's pumpkin pies, which I make now, pecan pie, and my aunt's oatmeal cake.

After the feast, the football fans wander into the bedroom for the games, the babies get put down for naps upstairs, and the rest of us commence work on the craft table upstairs in the playroom. Some years my sister provides supplies for a group project like painting aprons with fabric paint or working on a puzzle. Other years we return to the Thanksgiving Day project of our childhood: creating treats for the first Christmas tree, which is decorated outside for the wildlife. We roll pinecones in peanut butter and birdseed, string together cranberries and popcorn, tie garlands of peanuts in the shell, and fix pipe-cleaner handles on suet-filled orange halves. The small spruces and white pines we decorated as children are now taller than the house;

the lowest branches are above our heads. We find new, young pines for the honor these days, knowing that in a few years, both these trees and our children will be taller than we are.

My belly isn't the only thing that is satiated as the sun sets on this early winter day. As the last dish is wiped and put back into the china cabinet and the last group has gone into the cold night back to their own home, I feel full, not only of generations of recipes but also of memories of many years of this cherished and necessary tradition, of all the aunts, uncles, grand-mothers, and grandfathers who no longer occupy a physical place in the circle but have moved on to join the great cloud of witnesses to our gratitude. I am con-tented and nourished by the harvest of each other's shared blessings and burdens, grateful for the oppor-tunity to feast on the presence of each other and the testimony of God's faithfulness year after year, genera-tion after generation, season after season.

THANKSGIVING

I

"Aggressively flat," you say when I ask what you think
of it
We are driving north from Indianapolis
The farthest north you've ever been
I watch you as you try to catch
Each row of corn with your eye
"Like armies," you say, "like rows of soldiers
I never knew there were so many shades of brown."
You say, "It's really beautiful"
I glance over to see if you are sincere

II

The rain falls on your red Alabama clay
You are talking about football weather
And I am thinking that you were right
It does always feel like afternoon in Alabama
The cotton in the fields looks strange to me
Like snow that doesn't ever melt
You glance over to see if I am listening

III

I drive silently through Tennessee
You are waiting for me at the door
We bring our fields to one another
We both know about harvesting

PROMISE

Watch closely.
The earth will quietly, barely darken.
The days will shorten, not so you notice
At first, but then, when you wake,
You'll see the first-fruits of the change:
The leaves falling, suddenly yellow.
The heat will seem to press until
The moment it all at once sweetens,
And the rain that seemed so gone, so
Elsewhere, will arrive, bringing with it
What we forgot we needed,
but longed for all the same.

ACKNOWLEDGMENTS

Thanks to:

Jonathan. Thank you for asking me if I had a book in me. And thank you for sharing the process with me, and for being my friend.

Robert. Thank you for mentoring me and for thinking I "could write a sentence." You are one of my heroes.

Angela. Thank you for being willing to take a chance on me, and then being willing to push and pull me into better writing. I look forward to more.

Zondervan. Thanks for listening to Angela and for taking me on. I pray we hold each other up.

Home church. Thank you for being my support, my dumping ground, my sounding board, and my safe place. You are truly the Church in my life.

Suzanne (both of them), Holly, Corkie, Eileen, Maddison, Elizabeth, Grace, Sheree, Shelly, and Heather. Thank you for showing me what godly women look like, and how friends love each other.

My English friends. Thank you for welcoming me to your country and your hearts while I finished this book. You will always be a part of me.

Lee. Thank you for letting me work out my parenting on you; you are very forgiving. I love learning from you, and you make me very proud. "I love you, and there's nothing you can do about it."

Madeleine. Thank you for modeling grace and wisdom for your mother. You're the kid I want to be. "I love you, and there's nothing you can do about it."

Simon. Thank you for being my biggest fan. I'm yours too. You have the gift of happiness, and you spread it to everyone. "I love you, and there's nothing you can do about it."

Mom and Dad. Thank you for loving me and teaching me and for providing such a sound backdrop for my life story. And thank you for giving me a love of words. If I am writing my story, you are my soundtrack. I love you both more than I can say.

Andrew. For everything.